CO-OPERATION IN CHORLEY 1830-1880

A FALSE DAWN

John E. Harrison

Copyright © 2020 John E. Harrison.

All rights reserved. No part of this book may be reproduced, stored, or transmitted by any means—whether auditory, graphic, mechanical, or electronic—without written permission of the author, except in the case of brief excerpts used in critical articles and reviews. Unauthorized reproduction of any part of this work is illegal and is punishable by law.

ISBN: 978-1-6847-1859-7 (sc)
ISBN: 978-1-6847-1858-0 (e)

Library of Congress Control Number: 2020902356

Because of the dynamic nature of the Internet, any web addresses or links contained in this book may have changed since publication and may no longer be valid. The views expressed in this work are solely those of the author and do not necessarily reflect the views of the publisher, and the publisher hereby disclaims any responsibility for them.

Lulu Publishing Services rev. date: 09/03/2020

CONTENTS

Acknowledgements vii
Preface ix
Introduction xi

Chapter 1 The Co-operative Society of Silk and Calico
                Printers, Birkacre, and the beginnings of
                Co-operation 1
Chapter 2 Lancashire Co-operation from the 1830s to 1860 25
Chapter 3 A Second Coming:
                Co-operation in Chorley in the 1860s 37
Chapter 4 William Karfoot: A Chorley Co-operator and more ... 61
Chapter 5 The Chorley Co-operative Spinning and
                Manufacturing Company 71
Chapter 6 "Our Own", but serving the Community:
                The Co-operative Hall, Public Baths,
                Education and Housing 89
Chapter 7 The Decline of the Chorley Pilot Industrial
                Co-operative Society 101

Conclusions 127
Appendix: Co-operatives in Surrounding
                Townships 1860-80 131
Bibliography 147
Index 155
About the Author 159

ACKNOWLEDGEMENTS

I am indebted to the help I have received from the National Archives, the National Co-operative Archives in Manchester and the Working Class Movement Library in Salford, and from their able and helpful staff. My work owes much to Chorley Library and its microfilmed newspapers in the Community History Library and to the Lancashire County Library Service, through which I was able to access digital copies of old newspapers. Any mistakes are the sole responsibility of the Author.

I must thank former colleagues from Salford City Council, Jill Baker and Faith Mann who gave me the opportunity to get back to local history; to Dr. Andy Gritt, Dr. Stephen Caunce and the Institute of Local and Family History at the University of Central Lancashire for learning opportunities; to Chris Aspin and Peter Hampson; to Ian Bagshaw for help with two illustrations; to Peter Caterall for his photograph of Burgh Hall; to Jason Hurley of Crumplezone; to members of Chorley Historical and Archaeological Society for fellowship and support, and to my wife Christine and to my family for love and support and for indulging me.

PREFACE

We are in danger today of forgetting how important the Co-operative movement was in the nineteenth and twentieth centuries. There is a case that could be made that in the century following the establishment of the Co-op shop in Toad Lane, Rochdale, the Co-operative movement was the most successful enterprise in the country. Leaving aside its businesses, through its dividend system, its educational activities, its youth and women's activities and the Co-operative Party, it gave ordinary people a chance to shape their own lives. By 1950 it had twelve million members and as a mass organisation it dwarfed other mass member organisations such as the Labour Party, Trade Unions and even the Church of England.

My interest in this topic was triggered initially in 2008 by my attendance at a study day run by the Institute of Local and Family History at the University of Central Lancashire in Preston. The day focussed on different aspects of the Co-operative movement, but I was particularly taken by a talk on Co-operative Cotton Companies. Reference was made to there being such a company in Chorley, about which little was known

Like anyone who has studied nineteenth century Economic and Social History, I was aware of the main threads of Co-operative history; of the idealism of Robert Owen and of the later development of retail co-operation based on the successful model of the Rochdale Pioneers. But of Chorley I knew nothing, other than being aware that at one time there had been a Chorley Co-op, before it had been subsumed into larger and larger amalgamated Co-operative businesses.

A search of Chorley Library's Local Studies section led to the discovery of a piece of gold dust. This was Frank Longton's book "Fifty Years of Co-operation in Chorley 1887-1937", the Jubilee Souvenir of the Chorley Co-operative Society Limited. The book is typical of many such local Co-op histories produced by the CWS Printing Works at Reddish in Stockport to celebrate Jubilees and promote the aims of Co-operation. As such it is an uncritical account but contains valuable photographs of premises and members as well as data on numbers of members, share capital, sales and dividend and interest paid out. This, then, was the start of my researches into the early history of Co-operation in Chorley.

INTRODUCTION

Chorley in the nineteenth century evolved from being a small market town, to becoming an industrial town which still kept many of the features of a market town. Jim Heyes described it as being a "nucleus for a sub-region of neighbouring communities, among them Euxton, Coppull, Adlington, Whittle-le-Woods and more."[1] The process of evolution was not smooth and was in particular subject to the economic downturns which affected other towns in Lancashire and across the country. It was because of these economic fluctuations that, with the exception of Chorley itself, most communities in the sub-region also suffered population fluctuations.

The industrial base in Chorley was textiles, with not only spinning and weaving, but also printing, bleaching and dyeing works in and around the town. However, it was also part of the South Lancashire coal field and mining was an important industry and gave its own flavour to communities to the south and west of the town. The mixture of market town, cotton town and coal town gave Chorley characteristics which made it different from most other Lancashire towns and communities where Co-operation sought to grow.

This account of the early years of the Co-operative movement in Chorley sheds light on not only working-class history in nineteenth century Chorley, but also the wider history of Co-operation both in Lancashire and, in some respects, nationally.

---

[1] Heyes, Jim, 1994. A History of Chorley. Preston. 2.

The three businesses whose histories are described, all failed, but it is through failures that we learn. The story of Co-operative Production is not well known or understood and is often overlooked. Andrew Bibby's recent book on the Hebden Bridge mill has been a major advance in this area of study[2]. The story of retail co-operation, post Rochdale, going back to George Jacob Holyoake and subsequent historians, has tended to focus on growth and success with failure only coming into the story in the second half of the twentieth century.

My starting point was with Frank Longton's "Fifty Years of Co-operation in Chorley, 1887-1937". This commemorative history, like most histories of the co-operative movement, is bland and celebratory and tells the story of the Chorley Co-operative Society, its development and its successes. Longton briefly mentions earlier co-operative ventures which he describes as being relative failures by comparison with the Society that he was commissioned to commemorate. Also, by the twentieth century, interest was predominantly in retail co-operation, whereas two of the three early co-operative businesses in Chorley were non-retail. This book aims to provide a "prequel" to Longton's work.

Jim Heyes's "A History of Chorley" published in 1994, is in most respects an excellent town history, but does not touch on any aspect of Co-operative history. This oversight or marginalisation has become increasingly common, yet at one time the Co-operative Movement was a central feature of our towns. John Walton, in his article "Co-operation in Lancashire 1844-1914" argued that "the Co-op is fast becoming forgotten even in its own heartland."[3] Where, on other occasions, local historians have touched upon Co-operation, detail has been minimal and dates inaccurate. In respect of Birkacre, the co-operative period of the printworks history is largely ignored and the attempt to establish an Owenite co-operative community has not been touched upon by local historians.

Interestingly the Birkacre Co-operative has featured in Kirby

---

[2] Bibby Andrew, 2015. All Our Own Work. The Co-operative Pioneers of Hebden Bridge and their mill. London.

[3] Walton, John K., 1995. Co-operation in Lancashire 1844-1924 in North West Labour History.

and Musson's 1975 study of John Doherty, the trade unionist, radical and factory reformer in "The Voice of the People"[4], and in R G Garnett's 1972 book, "Co-operation and the Owenite Socialist Communities in Britain 1825-45."[5] Tantalisingly, A E Musson promised "a forthcoming article" which "will examine the Birkacre Project in more detail"[6], but I have found no evidence of this having been published.

Newspapers have been an important source material for my researches, ranging from Robert Owen's *The Crisis* and co-operative newspapers from the 1830s, 1860s and 1870s, to local reports in the Chorley and Preston papers. Generally lacking business records, it is from the newspapers that I have been able to draw figures on membership, sales and capital investment. The exception has been the information about shareholders and their investment in the Chorley Co-operative Spinning and Manufacturing Company submitted for registration as a joint stock venture. This information was obtained from the National Archive.

The members of these early co-operative societies have been always difficult to identify. The members of the Birkacre Society are presumed to have been mainly printers; more is known about the shareholders of Chorley Co-operative Mill by comparing names with census occupations; far less is known about the background of the Pilot Industrial Society's members. However, I have no reason to believe that, as in Firth's study of North East Lancashire, whilst there was extensive interaction with the "working class", some groups such as the poor and unskilled were more or less excluded.[7]

The fifty-year span of this book does not provide a continuous history as there is a huge gap in activity between the collapse of the Co-operative Printworks and the founding of the Chorley

---

[4] Kirby, R. G. and Musson, A. E., 1975. The Voice of the People; John Doherty, 1798-1854. Trade Unionist, radical and factory reformer. Manchester.
[5] Garnett, R. G., 1972. Co-operation and the Owenite socialist communities in Britain, 1825-45. Manchester.
[6] Kirby R. G. and Musson A E. Op. Cit. 344. Footnote 47.
[7] Firth, Peter, 1990. The Co-operative Movement and the Working Class in North East Lancashire 1870-1914. 1.

Pilot Industrial Co-operative Society. The town was a different community in 1860; the co-operators, whilst still having some Owenite aspirations, had been shaped by changes to society and the economy, and had aims which were perhaps more pragmatic, whilst still wishing to create a society, based on co-operative principles, that would better serve the needs of their members. This pragmatism is evidenced in setting up the Co-operative Mill as a joint stock company. As will be shown later, many co-operative historians today would not regard this as a true co-operative venture. I have chosen to include it because it was founded by co-operators and nearly eighty years after its foundation, Frank Longton in his history described it as a "co-operative production cotton mill" and wrote that it was an "attempt to put into practice the profit-sharing principle of co-operation".[8]

The concept of Co-operation in the 1860s and 1870s was more widely known and understood, and that is evidenced in the Chorley District by the foundation of retail societies in outlying communities. Ironically, though smaller businesses, they proved to be more sustainable than the co-operative businesses founded in Chorley in the early 1860s. In an appendix, I shall describe their early years and try to identify the driving forces in those communities that created village retail co-operatives.

---

[8] Longton, Frank, 1937. <u>Fifty Years of Co-operation in Chorley, 1887-1937.</u> Chorley Co-operative Society Limited.

1

The Co-operative Society of Silk and Calico Printers, Birkacre, and the beginnings of Co-operation

Long before the establishment of a co-operative printworks and community, Birkacre had been a significant part of the local and regional economy. In the eighteenth century Birkacre and Burgh had belonged to the Catholic Chadwick family. These estates, lying at the south western extremity of the Chorley township (being more than a mile from the town centre), were at the northern tip of the South Lancashire Coal Field, and there was a continuous history of mining in the area. This had been further encouraged by the Chadwicks with the development of forges and an iron-slitting mill at Birkacre on the banks of the River Yarrow.

Birkacre is on the northern bank of the River Yarrow and was where the river was crossed en route to Coppull, Standish and Wigan. In 1777 Richard Arkwright, inventor of the water frame and leading entrepreneur of the early industrial revolution, opened a cotton mill on the site of a forge there. He took an eighty-four year lease on the mill, the higher and lower forges, a corn mill, three weirs, a house and cottages, as well as a further thirteen and a half acres of land. Further industrial premises were added at an estimated cost of "upwards of £4,400"[9]. However, in 1779 the site was attacked and destroyed by a mob of between 4000 and 8000 men and women. They were seemingly disaffected textile workers and miners drawn from across southern Lancashire. Arkwright and his partners surrendered their lease in 1780 on the payment of £200, "thinking it insecure to proceed in their intended business in that place."[10] Birkacre was advertised for new tenants "for any branch where a large Head of Water is necessary, either in the cotton, linen or Printing business."[11]

Calico Printing had begun in Lancashire in the mid-1760s in Bamber Bridge and Oswaldtwistle, and it was as a printworks that the Birkacre site subsequently developed under various tenants. A sale after bankruptcy in 1782 described the business as "Birkacre House, Printing Shops, Warehouses and other buildings, seventeen cottages, and a water Corn Mill, and kiln, and 20 acres and 17 perches of land."[12] John Mellor took the lease from 1790 until his death in 1828, when he was found to be insolvent. "Creditors broke up the concern, was unoccupied for some years."[13]

As in the Bleaching industry, sites for calico printing factories were chosen in river valleys near reliable supplies of pure water. Although machine printing dated from 1783, when Thomas Bell of Walton-le-Dale took out a patent, block-printing was only gradually replaced. A description of the printing industry in the Manchester area (including Chorley) in 1846 showed that nearly all had printing tables for block-printing as well printing machines.[14] A trade directory in the 1790s listed six calico printers in Chorley, including John Mellor,[15] indicating that it was already an important industry in the district. An 1835 directory stated that the largest works were at Cowling Bridge, belonging to Messrs. Hole, Son and Watson, with smaller establishments at

---

[9] Fitton, R. S., 1989. <u>The Arkwrights, Spinners of Fortune.</u> Manchester. 51.
[10] House of Commons Journal, XXXVII, 926.
[11] Heyes, Jim. Op. Cit. 78.
[12] *Manchester Mercury* 8 October 1782.
[13] Graham, John. <u>The Chemistry of Calico Printing and History of Printworks in the Manchester District from 1760-1846.</u>
[14] Graham. Op. Cit.
[15] Universal British Directory Vol.2 Part2. 1793-98.

Birkacre, Adlington, Whittle and Brinscall. Collectively they gave "employment to a great number of workmen".[16] Cowling Bridge was situated on Black Brook. This fed the River Yarrow, which flows through Birkacre.

When the Birkacre Printworks re-opened in 1831, it was under the management of the Block Printers Union and their secretary, Ellis Piggot, and "conducted on what they considered the true principle for employing men."[17] That principle was Co-operation, and what was planned was not only a co-operative business, but a co-operative community.

Co-operation was a response to perceived exploitation of workers both in agriculture and in the new factory-based industries. Land enclosures and industrialization caused unprecedented changes throughout society in the late eighteenth and early nineteenth century. Wages were decreasing, short-time working and layoffs were frequent, and prices of basic commodities seemed to be always increasing. Dr. William King, an early advocate and propagandist for Co-operation expressed the situation thus:

> There are persons who think that.... the labourer can never be anything but a marketable commodity, to be bought and sold by capitalists, like a log of wood, a hat or a pig...
> The rate of wages has been gradually diminishing for some hundred years, so now it is not above one third of what it used to be ...the same causes, continuing to act, the wages must go on diminishing, till a workman will not be able to maintain a family; and by the same rule, he will at last not be able to maintain himself. This conclusion it is frightful to think of, but whether we think of it or not, it will march on in its own silent way, till it unexpectedly overwhelms us like a flood.[18]

---

[16] Robinson, C., 1835. An Historical and Descriptive Account of the Parish of Chorley. Chorley.15.
[17] Graham. Op Cit.
[18] Quoted in Birchall, Johnston, 1994. Co-op the people's business. Manchester. 7-8.

Responses to these changes were varied, and often violent. They included eighteenth century riots, the Luddite uprisings in Yorkshire and the East Midlands 1811-12, and the Swing Riots in Southern England in the late 1820s. Dr. King's response was non-violent, but part of the collective response to the

> frightening and seemingly amoral world being created by agricultural and industrial change, urbanization, and the emerging hegemony of the market.[19]

King's message was

> These evils can be cured: and the remedy is in our own hands. The remedy is CO-OPERATION.[20]

Early Co-ops were founded in Sheerness (1816), Brighton (1827) and London (1825), and by 1830 it was estimated that there were 266 societies.[21] The vast majority of these societies were retail businesses. However, for some this was not enough. As described by a nineteenth century historian of co-operative production:

> The sufferings endured by the large numbers thrown out of their employments, and the still larger numbers employed for excessive hours and at an immature age....caused many of the labouring classes, who remembered the "olden times", to wish for a state of society where the evils that they saw resulting from the use of machinery, and the adoption of the factory system, could be eliminated. Hence the many projects for self-supporting communities.[22]

---

[19] Wilson, John F., Webster Anthony, and Voberg- Rugh, Rachael, 2013. Building Co-operation, A Business History of the Co-operative Group, 1863-2013. Oxford. 25.
[20] Johnston Op. Cit. 9.
[21] Holyoake, George Jacob, 1875. The History of Co-operation in England, its Literature, and its Advocates Vol. 1. London. 153.
[22] Jones, B., 1894. Co-operative Production. Oxford. 47.

The main philosopher and supporter of co-operation at this time was Robert Owen.

Robert Owen as depicted at his memorial in Newtown, Powys.

Owen not only shared the ideas of William King, he was the main source. Owen had been a successful mill owner at New Lanark in Scotland, and was one of the most enlightened employers of that time. He believed that human character "was formed for people, out of the environment in which they had to live,"[23] and therefore, at New Lanark he provided community rooms, housing, public halls and educational facilities. Based on this experience he developed the belief that

> given the right environment, people could form co-operative communities, "villages of co-operation" just like New Lanark, which would solve the problem of poverty by allowing working-class people to opt out of capitalist society into a "New Moral World" in which they would grow their own food, make their own clothes and eventually (under Mr. Owen's careful guidance) become self-governing.[24]

---

[23] Johnston Op. Cit. 20.
[24] Johnston Op. Cit. 20.

Community building attracted

> The largest practical commitment of the Owenite movement, measured by the amount of time, effort and capital involved.....The community, or Village of Co-operation was the central institution of Owenism.[25]

Eventually, with the help of wealthy supporters he began to form communities, at Orbiston in Scotland and New Harmony in the USA. After a few years both communities failed. His were not the only communities established at this time. A small community near Exeter took over six acres of land in 1826, but failed when a financial backer withdrew his capital[26].

The importance of Robert Owen, despite the impractical nature of his plans was that he communicated profound underlying values. He believed that "the right to a full humanity was to be available to all, even to the humble peasant and cotton spinner and street sweeper."[27] He believed that by creating a non-competitive environment, civilised behaviour would grow up naturally. His philosophy was taken up by more practical co-operators. They were inspired by Owen but did not necessarily copy him.

Whether Ellis Piggott and his colleagues would have described themselves as Owenites, it is not possible to say. In many respects his roots seem to be more in trade unionism. Piggott's Block Printers Union was only formed in 1830. He was also the innkeeper where the Manchester delegate conference was held in June 1830 and a registered owner of the newspaper *The Voice*.[28] This newspaper was principally the propaganda vehicle for John Doherty, the leading trade unionist of this period, and his trade union, The National Association for the Protection of Labour. *The Voice* was a weekly newspaper and was first published on the 31st December 1830.

---

[25] Harrison, J. F. C., 1969. Robert Owen and the Owenites in Britain and America-The Quest for the New Moral World. London. 163.
[26] Garnett, R. G. Op. Cit. 50.
[27] Pollard S., and Salt, J., 1971. Robert Owen: Prophet of the Poor. Lewisburg.x.
[28] Kirby and Musson. Op. Cit. 225.

Although the Piggott link to Birkacre is a strong one, a direct link between Doherty and the Birkacre Printworks Co-operative has yet to be established. However, the National Association for the Protection of Labour was supported in Chorley, and Doherty spoke at meetings in Chorley around this time on more than one occasion. Donations from Chorley Spinners to the National Association were recorded in the period from July 1830 to March 1831.[29] At the first delegate conference of the National Association held in Manchester in June 1830, twenty-eight delegates attended, representing nine districts, one of which was Chorley.[30] On the 29th November 1830, Doherty addressed a meeting in Chorley

> on the importance of the Association and the necessity of establishing their own newspaper. His audience consisted mostly of members of the local political union.[31]

The political issues of that audience were addressed when he returned to Chorley the following year when he spoke at a meeting supporting electoral reform.[32] When the fifth General Delegate Conference was held again in Manchester in June 1831, amongst the twenty delegates were representatives of Chorley and neighbouring communities in Preston, Blackrod and Bolton.[33]

That Doherty and his National Association had support in Chorley is not surprising. In 1826 Chorley was visited by William Cobbett, the political reform campaigner, who was standing for election for parliament in Preston,[34] and subsequently an address from residents of Chorley to the electors of Preston was published and circulated:

---

[29] Kirby and Musson. Op. Cit. 113.
[30] Kirby and Musson. Op. Cit. 168.
[31] Kirby and Musson. Op. Cit. 189.
[32] Kirby and Musson. Op. Cit. 428.
[33] Kirby and Musson. Op. Cit. 241.
[34] Cobbett's Weekly *Political Register* 27 May 1826.

Gentlemen, we, the unrepresented part of the inhabitants of Chorley and its vicinity, beg leave to address you on the subject of the ensuing election.

We have seen you struggling against the monstrous coalition for the last twenty years with admiration and sympathy. We congratulate you on this bursting of your fetters. We congratulate you on the grand opportunity you now have of sending the only real champion of the people, Mr. Cobbett, into Parliament.[35]

Preston was a centre of radicalism. In 1820, Henry "Orator" Hunt, who gained fame from Peterloo, received 1,127 votes out of a male electorate of just over 6,000, and in 1830 he was successful in achieving a majority.

Cobbett was one of the most charismatic political reformers of that period. He saw himself as being the champion of the labouring classes. Quite possibly he saw Chorley as being fertile territory, as earlier in the year, in April 1826, Chorley was one of the towns attacked by the East Lancashire loom breakers. The attack had started from Tockholes, eight miles away, and had picked up support from the communities it had passed along the way. Their target was the Water Street mill of Thomas Lightoller and William Harrison which had power looms. The owners were "known as hard and unscrupulous employers,[36]" and had previously been convicted of employing children under eight years of age and making children under sixteen work for more than twelve hours a day. The leaders of the attack were not from Chorley but many of the townsfolk "were sympathetic and prepared to help if necessary.......a great multitude of the townspeople outside were their friends."[37] Eighty powerlooms were destroyed. The Lightollers were again targeted in 1830 during

---

[35] Cobbett's Weekly *Political Register* 10 June 1826.
[36] Turner, William, 1992. Riot! The Story of the East Lancashire Loom-Breakers in 1826. Preston.55.
[37] Turner. Op. Cit. P 58. Quoting from the *Preston Advertiser* 29 April 1826.

a spinners' dispute when a canister of gunpowder was lowered down the chimney of the mill house causing "a violent explosion."[38]

The Calico Printers Union pre-dated the Cotton Spinners' Union. "For nearly thirty years after, and despite the Combination Acts (passed in 1800/01), they remained one of the strongest and complete of unions"[39], and they operated on a national scale. Twenty years after the founding of the Birkacre Co-operative, the Block Printers published their policy on Co-operation:

> We believe the great cause of human misery is the disunion, in the proprietorship, of capital, skill, and labour; consequently, if we are right, the remedy consists in uniting them........Perhaps we have waited too long; if so we must wait no longer. We may wait on the banks of the great and ever-growing river of poverty, for the golden boat of the Capitalist to carry us over, till we perish of starvation.[40]

John Doherty was principally a trade unionist and political agitator, and initially was not a supporter of co-operation. When in 1830, during a debate in the National Association for the Protection of Labour on a rule to safeguard funds, a delegate from the calico printers favoured putting the money into a co-operative scheme, Doherty ridiculed the idea.[41] He was not an Owenite, and disagreements between co-operators and trades unionists were common at this time, particularly about the remedies to the social and economic ills that affected the labouring classes. Nonetheless, by 1830 the concept of co-operation was becoming more widely known and supported. Seventeen co-operative societies were founded in 1829, fifteen in 1830 and twelve in 1832.[42] Many of

---
[38] *Bury and Norwich Post.* 16 June 1830.
[39] Turner, H. A., 1962. Trade Union Growth, Structure and Policy- A Comparative Study of the Cotton Unions. London.57.
[40] Organization of Labour: Report of Committee appointed 6 September 1851 to consider and devise the best method of carrying out the Block-Printers' desire of Trades' Co-operation into effect. Paisley. 1851. 4.
[41] Kirby and Musson. Op. Cit. 169.
[42] Garnett. Op. Cit. 134.

these were in Lancashire; most were retail, but a few were for co-operative production. In 1851 *The Christian Socialist* published extracts from the first issue of *The Co-operator* in 1828, setting out the principle of these early societies;

> That of accumulating a common capital, and investing it in trade, and so making 10% of it, instead of investing it in the funds, at only four or four and a half, with the intention of ultimately purchasing land, and living in COMMUNITY.[43]

A pivotal event, in March 1830, leading to a modifying of Doherty's views on Co-operation, and probably helping to promote the Birkacre Co-op, was a series of lectures given in Manchester by William Pare, the Birmingham co-operative missionary. He argued that the only solution to society's ills was co-operative production and exchange of goods, leading ultimately to a co-operative community. Pare argued that Trade Unions had failed in their efforts to maintain wage levels and they should seek to replace the competitive system by investing their funds in co-operative societies.[44] In response, Doherty declared his support for "the beautiful system" of co-operation. This may well have been the endorsement that Ellis Piggott and the Block Printers Union required. It would have been far more desirable to take over an existing site, albeit one that had not been operational for a couple of years, rather than to build "from scratch".

At the First Co-operative Congress, held in Manchester on the 26th and 27th May 1831, there was strong support for co-operative communities. In an address to societies it was argued that

> Co-operation seeks to put the Working Classes in that situation where they shall enjoy the whole produce of their labour, instead of the small part

---

[43] *The Co-operator*. No1. 1 May 1828, copied in *The Christian Socialist*. 11 October 1851.
[44] Kirby and Musson. Op. Cit.324.

called "wages". This can be done only by the establishment of Communities.[45]

The Birkacre Co-operative reported to the First Congress that it had funds of £4,000 and employed 150 members. [46]However it seems that the society was not yet operative as it was later reported that the "Co-operative Society of Silk and Calico Printers, Birkacre, Lancashire", "entered upon" the premises on the 29th September 1831.[47] Whether this was the official title of the Society is unclear, as it is not repeated in other contemporary reports. However, as no other name has been found for this business, it is the one that I have chosen to use in the title of this chapter.

The same report gives a description of whole estate which had been taken on.

> The estate of Birkacre, consists of 54 statute acres, out of which 14 acres are occupied by reservoirs, the works are calculated for 108 tables, and 4 machines, which will employ 450 hands. There is one corn mill on the works with three pairs of stones, with a good supply of water, likewise there are 29 cottages...The numbers of members are 300. The sum belonging to the society is £400. The society manufactures Calicoes, Muslins, Silks, Palmareens, Valences, Terenetts, Battistes, Bombazines, Woollens etc.[48]

This would appear to be a larger estate, in terms of acreage, than that advertised in the 1780s with twelve more cottages. Given that the site was so far out from the centre of Chorley, the cottages would be needed to attract workers and their families, although insufficient for a business aiming to employ 450.

At the second congress it was reported that the Birkacre

---

[45] Co-operative Congress Reports and Papers. 1831-2.
[46] Garnett. Op. Cit. 134.
[47] *The Lancashire and Yorkshire Co-operator.* No. 7. 15.
[48] Ibid. 15.

Calico Printers Society had capital of £1,000.[49] This appears to be more realistic and the figure of £4,000 reported to the first congress may well have been a typographical error, given the later report of starting capital of £400. However, all reported statistics should be regarded with caution, as there is a tendency for enthusiastic propagandists to exaggerate.

One of the propagandists who reported about the Society both to the Co-operative Congress and to Robert Owen was William Carson. Carson was one of the leading supporters of co-operation in Lancashire. He came from Wigan and in 1831 provided a description of the foundation of a co-operative society in Wigan in 1830. He was described as the President of that society.[50] Along with Edmund Taylor, who appears to have been a Chorley man, he represented the Birkacre Co-operative at the second Co-operative Congress. When he addressed the fourth Co-operative Congress on the 1st October 1832, he described himself as "having been instrumental in forming a great number of societies."[51] At that congress he was also referred to as a trustee of the North West of England United Co-operative Company. This had been set up in August 1831 at the instigation of Robert Owen at the first Congress. This company was to fulfil a wholesale function for retail societies, selling at near to cost prices, and an outlet for goods manufactured co-operatively. The proceeds of the business were to be used to help fund a co-operative community.

Carson provided the fullest description of the Birkacre community and business in a letter to Robert Owen, dated the 1st March 1832, when he described himself as being "Clerk of Works at New Church, Wigan". The letter starts with a request for advice from Owen about founding a boarding school for 500 pupils in the North of England. He then moves on to inform Owen of other developments, including Birkacre:

> Myself and Mr. Hirst visited the Birkacre Co-operative Print Works last week, when we found them as busy as a hive of bees. Millwrights, Smiths,

---
[49] Garnett Op. Cit.136.
[50] *Lancashire Co-operator*. No. 1. 11 June 1831. 2-3.
[51] *The Crisis*. Vol. 1. No. 34. 135.

Masons, Carpenters, Labourers, Block and Machine Makers, Printers, Cutters, Drawers, Colour Makers, Engineers, Madder Dyers and Crofters, all at work in their different departments. The first seen was a quantity of men turning a large house that had formerly been vacated by a Large Manufacturer into convenient apartments for themselves.; to this house is attached (writing unclear) fish ponds, and beautifully cut serpentine walks; and the millwright was putting up a New Iron Water Wheel 24 feet diameter, length of bucket 8 feet; the (writing unclear) putting up machinery for printing; the printers at work..some beautiful new pattern silks, cottons, and they have already laid out £2,000 on the premises which (h)as been subscribed in 6d and shillings. They have about 120 acres of Pasture Land, about 6 of which is Water. On the Estate is one Corn Mill and 30 Cottages. They pay £600 per year rent and have Factory Room with necessary apparatus for 400 Men. There is now about 100 at work and as soon as their machinery is finished, they will fill the factory. They have the most skilful mechanics in all the different branches picked out from thousands to conduct and instruct their Brothers. There is no Mastership, no rivalling one another. All is Peace and Brotherhood. They have their agent in the Market and have more orders than they can supply- all their patterns are entirely new. I could tell you much more but my paper will not permit (at the bottom of the page).[52]

Thomas Hirst, who accompanied William Carson on his visit to Birkacre, was another leading figure in the Co-operative movement at this time. He was from Huddersfield, was a trustee of the North West of England United Co-operative Company, and chaired meetings of the Fourth Co-operative Congress in October

---

[52] Letter to Robert Owen from Mr. Carson of Haigh. 1 March 1832. Letter 522 in Robert Owen's Correspondence.

1832. He led "Co-operative Missionary Tours", and his third tour was to Manchester, Stockport, Warrington, Birkacre, Eccles and Bolton.[53] He appeared to have made a further visit

> In the early part of August (1832), Mr. Hirst, on his way to Kendal, informs us he called at BIRKACRE, and that he is happy to state that he found the establishment, as far as he was able to judge, in a very prosperous state, and the members of one heart and one mind.[54]

This interest in Birkacre by national figures in the Co-operative Movement reflects the importance of the project. Musson described Birkacre as" the most important attempt at co-operative production during the early Owenite period."[55] It was, for example, a much larger concern than the Co-operative Dyeing business at Hulme in Manchester, which employed nearly seventy. A report about this business stated that "in this establishment, as well as that of BIRKACRE, we have a practical example that poor men *can* manage their own affairs."[56] Birkacre, however, in a statistical return to the Second Co-operative Congress was claimed to have 3,000 members, of whom 150 were employed, and £4,000 in funds. It was perhaps the scale of the Birkacre project which focussed the attention of the Co-operative Movement, and beyond.

At the third Co-operative Congress Birkacre and Ralahine were praised as the most successful of the Co-operative ventures.[57] (Ralahine was an Owenite experiment with a strong agricultural focus in County Clare, Ireland that ran between 1831 and 1833.)

To be successful, the business had to produce and sell its products. It was reported to the Second Co-operative Congress that the Birkacre Calico Printers Society had been promised £300 in

---

[53] *The Lancashire and Yorkshire Co-operator* No. 1. 6.
[54] *The Lancashire and Yorkshire Co-operator.* September 1832. 13.
[55] Musson, A. E., 1974. Trade Union and Social History, London. 173.
[56] *The Lancashire and Yorkshire Co-operator* August 1832.13.
[57] Garnett. Op. Cit.138.

weekly purchases from the Liverpool Co-operative Company.[58] This probably was a shorthand reference to the North West of England United Co-operative Company. It was founded in Liverpool in 1831 with Carson as a trustee. The congresses gave an opportunity for producer societies to display their wares. At the Fourth Congress held in Liverpool at the King's Arms Hotel, the Assembly Room had been converted to a "bazaar" for the purpose of selling co-operative manufactured produce. There were woollen cloths from Huddersfield, linens from Barnsley, ribbons from Coventry, flannels and blankets from Rochdale, shoes from Kendal, tools from Sheffield, and printed cottons from Birkacre.[59]

In the various reports about the Birkacre Co-operative Printworks there is little consistency in the figures provided for the site, the number of members and the number of workers. Arkwright leased thirteen and a half acres of land, but when advertised for sale in 1782, the site was twenty acres seventeen perches; the Tithe Map ledger from the late 1830s when the site was managed by George and Samuel Potter, gave an acreage of just over twenty nine.[60] Carson in his letter to Robert Owen wrote "They have about 120 acres of Pasture Land about 6 of which is Water."[61] Yet the report in the Lancashire and Yorkshire Co-operator stated "The estate of Birkacre consists of 54 statute acres out of which 14 acres are occupied by reservoirs."[62] This may be the more accurate figure as when the Print works were offered for sale in 1834, they were described as "Print and Bleach Works, reservoirs, and premises situate at Birkacre, near Chorley, with about fifty acres of meadow and pasture land."[63]

The explanation for the difference between these figures must lie in the inclusion of a large neighbouring estate in the Co-operative project. This was probably Burgh Hall, which like Birkacre was owned by Thomas Watts. In 1824 the Burgh and Birkacre estate was sold by the Chadwick Trustees to James

---

[58] Garnett. Op. Cit. 136.
[59] Proceedings of the Fourth Congress.1832.1.
[60] Chorley Tithe Map. Lancashire County Record Office. DRB 1/43.
[61] Letter to Robert Owen from Mr. Carson of Haigh. Op. Cit.
[62] *Lancashire and Yorkshire Co-operator* No.7
[63] *Manchester Times and Gazette* 14 June 1834.

John E. Harrison

Anderton and passed to his sons, and son-in-law Thomas Watts. James Anderton was described in 1824 as a Cotton Spinner, living in St. Thomas's Square, Chorley.[64] The following map shows the position of Burgh Hall and woods vis a vis Birkacre.

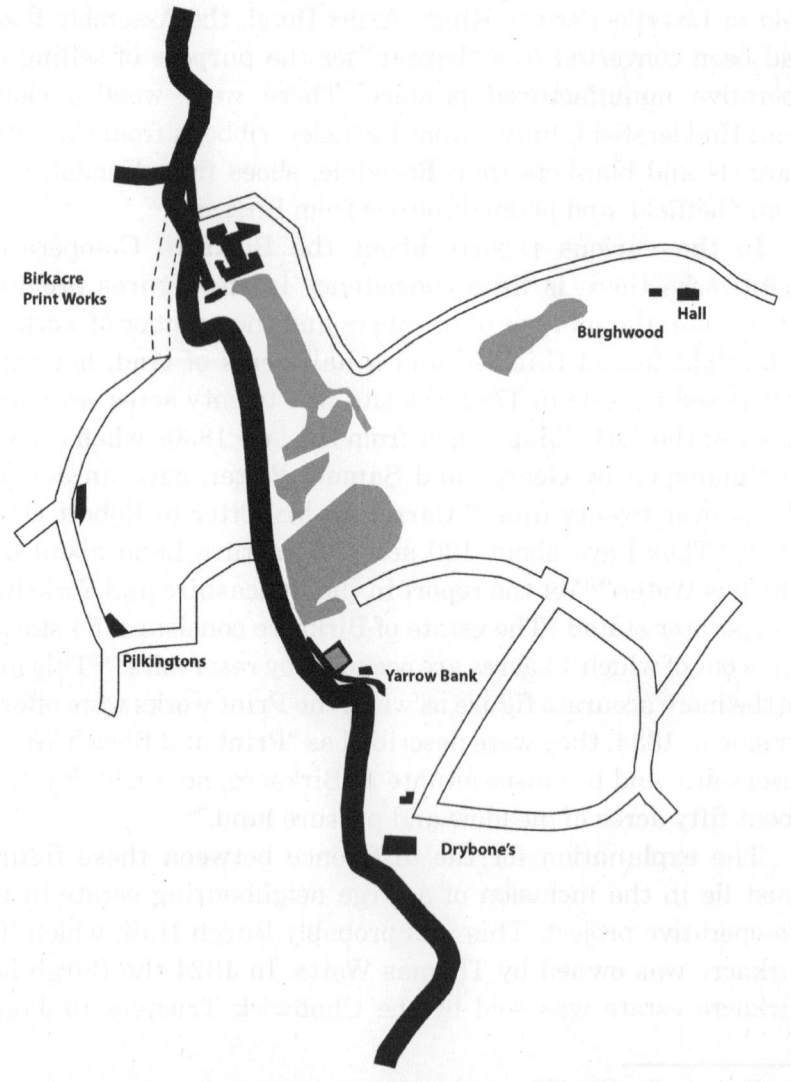

Birkacre and Burgh

---

[64] Baines Lancashire Directory Vol. 1 1824.

The corroboration for this is to be found in Carson's description

> a large house that had formerly been occupied by a Large Manufacturer..to this house is attached.. fish ponds and beautifully cut serpentine walks.[65]

He developed this further when addressing the third Co-operative Congress in 1832:

> They have now an estate which once belonged to a large cotton lord, and a mansion now turned into dwellings for the poor......the large drawing room of this cotton lord, which was too extensive for the wants of the humble mechanics, has been despoiled of its ornamental trappings, and divided into two conveniently sized apartments.[66]

Carson's descriptions are more redolent of Burgh Hall than Birkacre House, which was situated in the middle of the Printworks. An 1835 Directory for Chorley describes Burgh Hall as

> a plain substantial brick building..(which) partakes much of the modern style of architecture....The pleasure grounds and gardens are well adapted to please the eye....In summer the thick foliage of the woods which shades the walks and grounds, imparts to the place an air of quiet and retirement.[67]

The following is a photograph of Burgh Hall in the 1970s before it was demolished.

---

[65] Letter to Robert Owen from Mr. Carson. Op. Cit.
[66] Third Co-operative Congress 1832.33.
[67] Robinson, C. Op, Cit.6.

John E. Harrison

Burgh Hall

The addition of the Burgh estate would also explain figures for cottages included in the co-operative. When the works were advertised for sale in 1782, there were seventeen cottages; the 1834 sale referred to "about 26 cottages". Carson writing to Robert Owen gives a figure of thirty, yet when reporting to the Co-operative Congress stated "Upon this estate there are sixty cottages, which are all turned to a good and profitable account."[68]

A less charitable view would argue that co-operators perhaps had a tendency to exaggerate in their enthusiasm. There is evidence for this in the information provided about the business's capital, subscribers and workforce. The Lancashire and Yorkshire Co-operator reported

> The number of members are 300. The sum belonging to the society is £400. The sum subscribed by the members of the Society is £500.[69]

As this immediately followed "The premises were entered upon 29 September 1831", it would seem to be a description of the start-up position. However, the First Co-operative Congress

---

[68] *The Crisis.* 28 April 1832.
[69] *The Lancashire and Yorkshire Co-operator.* No. 7. 15.

was advised by the Birkacre co-operative that it had £4,000 in funds with 150 members employed.[70] By the Second Congress (4-6 October 1831), capital was £1,000, membership 1,500 (3,000 at the first congress). Carson still referred to 3,000 members at the Third Congress in 1832;[71] that figure was repeated at the Fourth Congress later in the year when Edmund Taylor, the Birkacre representative "of a society of 3,000 members", gave details of the Society.[72]

It is futile 180 years later to try to fix a precise figure for membership. However, it would certainly appear to be considerable, undoubtedly drawing on the members of Ellis Piggott's Block Printworker's Union from beyond Chorley and District and across the country.

What did they understand that they were subscribing to? Calico Printers had been involved in various strikes and were unhappy with industrial relations. There was considerable support for producer co-operatives, but Birkacre led the way in terms of providing co-operative production as part of a co-operative community.

Of the workforce, little is known. The figure of 150 employed members given to the First Co-operative Congress may well have included workers preparing the site and premises. Carson implied this in his letter to Robert Owen. He referred to "Factory Room with necessary apparatus for 400 men. There is now about 100 at work and as soon as their machinery is finished, they will fill the factory."[73] Edmund Taylor's figures, "between thirty and forty journeymen calico printers constantly at work" seems like a reliable figure.[74] Given that the site had been used for printing for over forty years, there may well have been a core of skilled workers living locally who had worked for the previous management. Workers from other local printworks may have been attracted particularly if trade had been difficult. The Crosse Hall Printworks, also known as Cowling Bridge, on Black Brook,

---

[70] Garnett Op. Cit.134.
[71] Third Co-operative Congress 1832 33.
[72] *The Crisis*. Vol.1 No. 34. 27 October 1832. 135.
[73] Letter to Robert Owen from Mr. Carson. Op, Cit.
[74] *The Crisis*. Vol. 1 No. 34. October 27 1832. 135.

to the east of Chorley, had been started in 1786 and experienced various business fluctuations, including a two-year closure. It was eventually taken on successfully by Richard Cobden.

Carson told Owen that "they have the most skilful mechanics",[75] but the quality of the workmanship was severely criticised by John Graham, writing a history of printworks in the 1840s. "The cloth was often tendered and the work generally bad."[76]

The cost of fitting out the printworks and its associated premises must have been considerable, not least because creditors had broken up the business after John Mellor's death in 1828. The notice of sale in 1834 stated that "Part of the print works have been lately erected....and fitted up in the best manner with all necessary new gearing."[77] Carson told Robert Owen that the co-operative "had already laid out £2,000 on industrial premises." In addition, £600 was to be paid in annual rent.[78] Unlike some other Owenite communities, there is no record of any financial backer to the scheme. The bulk of the capital must have been provided by the members. Carson referred to subscriptions in pounds and shillings, and Edmund Taylor to the first pound being laid down.

The capital was needed and used to create the whole community. In addition to the industrial premises, land and accommodation, the Birkacre Community was provided with a library, reading room and school. Carson reported that

> It is indeed a glorious sight to see these men enjoying themselves during their leisure hours, by bodily recreation and mental amusement.....they are now placed in an independent situation – morally as well as physically- and far, very far above want. Their families are healthful and cheerful, their bodies clothed and their appetites satisfied, by means of industry and perseverance.[79]

---

[75] Letter Op. Cit.
[76] Graham, John. Op. Cit.
[77] *Manchester Times and Gazette* 14 June 1834.
[78] Letter to Robert Owen from Mr. Carson. Op. Cit.
[79] *The Crisis.* Vol. 1 No. 4. 28 April 1832.

The education provision was an important Owenite provision to enable members to participate in the running of co-operative communities. It was suggested that members should contribute their own small collections of books. Charles Fry, a leading figure in the Liverpool Co-operative Wholesale Purchasing Agency, and probably known to Carson wrote to the *Liverpool Mercury* in 1828:

> I trust that all co-operative societies have a library attached to them, and the members are making the books that they may each possess useful to their brother co-operators.[80]

Sadly, these halcyon days did not last. "An experimental approach implied there would be trial and error, not necessarily success."[81] Few of these early co-operatives lasted more than two or three years. Birkacre was no exception to this rule. In October 1833 the *London Gazettes* reported the bankruptcy of G Fairbrother and T Williams of Birkacre, Lancashire, Calico Printers.[82] This must have been the Co-operative business. The Printworks were up for sale in June 1834. There are no further records or reports of the Birkacre Co-op after the 1st October 1832 when it was represented at the Fourth Co-operative Congress in Liverpool by Edmund Taylor and Thomas Yates. With hindsight, Taylor's speech to the congress can be seen as showing that early idealism had come face to face with some realism;

> Mr. E. Taylor, of Birkacre, said he had heard much about Community, but he thought a great many who took the subject up, did so very rashly. (Hear, hear) They talked of getting on the land, but said little of the principles which they were to associate. Their

---

[80] Everitt, Jean, 1997. Co-operative Society Libraries and Newsroom of Lancashire and Yorkshire from 1844 to 1918. D. Phil thesis. University of Wales., Aberystwyth.93.
[81] Harrison, J. F. C. Op. Cit. 176.
[82] *Lancaster Gazetter* 26 October 1833. NB. George Fairbrother, Calico Printer married in Bolton le Moors in 1812. Thomas Williams was a calico printer employing 20 men at Ainsworth Mill, near Bury in the 1851 census.

minds were not sufficiently matured, and it would in his opinion, be productive of much mischief to endeavour to form a community whilst this was the case. They must be prepared to act unanimously and harmoniously or their ends would be defeated. (Hear, hear).[83]

Birkacre became one the "Lost Communities". The description was given by George Jacob Holyoake, the Co-operative Movement's first historian, to the failed Owenite experiments of this period. He wrote that

> No social community in Great Britain had a long enough time allowed to give it a reasonable chance of succeeding...Establishing a new world is naturally a more elaborate and protracted work than establishing a new manufacture.[84]

He suggested that there were two reasons for the failure of many of the communities.

> First: The want of sufficient capital to maintain the place for a few years on a frugal scale until the members could be trained in self-supporting efficiency. Second: Members were not picked men, nor pledged to obey the authority established over them.[85]

J F C Harrison agreed that "the raising of capital to commence a community was perhaps the crucial issue."[86] Where subscriptions and shares were not adequate, the generosity of landed proprietors or large capitalists were relied on. At Birkacre, in addition to funding the initial financial outlay, income needed to be generated from members and/or sales to meet the £600 per

---

[83] Fourth Co-operative Congress. 1832. P 29.
[84] Holyoake, George Jacob. Op. Cit. 317.
[85] Holyoake. Op. Cit. 166
[86] Harrison, J. F. C. Op. Cit. 180.

annum rental. William Carson described that as "an enormous sum."[87] The contract to supply the co-operative business in Liverpool may have been sufficient alone to generate sufficient income; it may not have been matched elsewhere.

Other factors could have been important. Reference has been made earlier to John Graham's serious criticism of the quality of the product. Graham went on to write

> When a 3 or 4 OVER would have done, they cut it for a 6 or 8 OVER. Knew a man HORROCKS, a machine printer who worked day work printed 9 pieces and drew £13 took some copper rollers off the works to pay himself.[88]

This may well illustrate lax and inefficient management, although I wonder if Horrocks's sale of the copper rollers occurred when he knew the business was failing and feared for his payment.

The Co-operator, writing about the failure of co-operative businesses founded between 1828 and 1830, offered four reasons[89];

1. Want of education among the working classes.
2. Societies being turned into means of political agitation.
3. Some members not continuing to deal at their own co-operative shop, while others got into debt.
4. Want of business habits among the managing committee.

The failure of the business may have had less to do with its co-operative nature and more to do with national factors such as the fluctuations of the economy or the attacks on trade unions by employers. Turnbull and Southern suggest that the closure of many early societies in Lancashire and elsewhere from 1834 onwards was due to the onset of a national economic depression. However, the extent to which that depression was

---

[87] *The Crisis*. Vol. 1. No. 4. 28 April 1832.
[88] Graham. Op. Cit.
[89] *Christian Socialist*. Vol. II. 260-1. 25 October 1851

reflected in Chorley at this time is not known,[90] and the fact that the printworks appeared to be operating again under the new management of Wardley and Hodson by 1835, would seem to make a serious trade depression as the main cause of failure, less likely.[91]

Doherty was sufficiently concerned about the counter-attacks by employers that in the autumn of 1833 he composed an address "To the Operative Calico- Printers and Others of England". It was written on behalf of Scottish printers who were on strike and their masters had advertised for new hands in England.[92] Perhaps they recruited printers from Birkacre.

All the above to varying degrees may have been factors in the failure of the Birkacre Co-op. In addition, it would seem as if there were mixed agendas. Carson, the Owenite was clearly driven by the wish to create a freestanding community. The Block Printers seemed to start from a position of establishing co-operative production to escape from the worst of the new industrial system and its capitalists. Taylor's speech to the Fourth Co-operative Congress seems to suggest that there may not have been widespread understanding and support of going beyond the Co-operative Printworks to create a Co-operative Community.

---

[90] Turnbull, Jean and Southern, Jayne, 1995. More than a Shop. A History of the Co-op in Lancashire. Lancashire.1.
[91] Robinson. Op. Cit. 15.
[92] Kirby and Musson. Op. Cit. 275.

2

Lancashire Co-operation from the 1830s to 1860

With the collapse of the Birkacre Co-operative venture in the early 1830s, although Co-operation continues to develop in other parts of the country, there is a hiatus in the history of co-operation in Chorley and District until the foundation of the Chorley Pilot Industrial Co-operative Society in 1860. Undoubtedly for most people in Chorley the struggles of daily life were the priority, but in addressing those struggles, there were benefits in working together. The cost of funerals and burials has always been a concern as working people ensure a "decent burial" for a deceased relative. In 1834, handloom weavers in Bolton Street formed the Chorley Family Funeral and Friendly Assurance Society. In its first year the Society's membership reached 1010.

The growth of the Funeral Society reflects the demographic and economic growth of the town. At the start of the 1830s a trade directory described Chorley as "one of the most thriving and agreeable places in the country," and recorded a great increase in houses and inhabitants.[93] It remained the main market town for the area, but it had an expanding industrial base. This base was largely textile focussed and susceptible to trade fluctuations and depressions. By 1838 the town had nine cotton manufacturers

---

[93] Pigot, James and Co., 1830. New Commercial Directory for the Counties of Cheshire, Derbyshire and Lancashire. Manchester.

employing 1800 hands as well as five coal mines[94]. The arrival of the Bolton to Preston Railway in the early 1840s was in part in response to this industrial expansion and served to further accelerate growth. Railways were joint stock ventures and their success prompted support for other similar investments. In 1845 Joint Stock Cotton Companies were formed in both Chorley and Leyland.[95] As will be seen in the following chapters, the joint stock model impacted on the development of co-operation in Chorley. The industrial growth led the town's population to increase by 36% between 1831 and 1851. This was largely achieved by immigration in part from the surrounding villages but also from further afield, including Ireland.

This was a period of tremendous change and unrest. There was an emergence of a distinct working-class culture. This had various roots which were not the same in all communities. However, it did draw on a shared experience of the Industrial Revolution. Hobsbawm has argued that "No period of British history has been as tense, as politically and socially disturbed, as the 1830s and early 1840s."[96]

Many working-class people were disappointed with the failure of the 1832 Reform Act to give them the vote and were bitterly opposed to the New Poor Law of 1834. Local and regional Trade Unions continued to be formed. Industrial action was frequent, but progress in terms of improved pay and working conditions appears to have been minimal.

A political Union had been formed in Chorley in 1830 and in 1833 the *Poor Man's Guardian* published a letter from Lawrence Garstang reporting that at a recent "numerous" meeting of the Chorley National Union "it was unanimously agreed that this meeting has no confidence in the present ministers, neither do we expect any good from the reformed parliament."[97]

On the moral front, Chorley had involvement with teetotalism from an early stage. Joseph Livesey gave his malt lecture in

---

[94] Butterworth, Edwin, 1841. A Statistical Sketch of the County Palatine of Lancaster, Manchester.
[95] *Preston Chronicle.* 4 October 1845 and 18 October 1845.
[96] Hobsbawm E. J., 1968. Industry and Empire. London. 77.
[97] *Poor Man's Guardian.* 9 March 1833.

Preston in 1833, but his first tract, "The Besetting Sin" was printed in Chorley in 1825. A Temperance Hotel opened in 1833 and a Temperance Society was formed.[98]

The social, economic and industrial turmoil was clearly seen by local landowners as extremely threatening and potentially de-stabilising. One of their responses was to form the Chorley Operative Conservative Association. *The Times* reported at great length on a dinner and procession at Chorley in the 24th November 1836 edition. The meeting was chaired by the Lord of the Manor and was supported by the leading landowners and churchmen. It was claimed that membership of the Association numbered 300 and that its foundation proved the independence of the working classes. Most of the proceedings were toasts and responses to the various pillars of the constitution and establishment, led by landowners and churchmen. The creation of the Association was opposed by the Whig-supporting local industrialists in a manifesto which illustrated a clear division in the town.[99] That division was between landowners and industrialists, but in the following year a different division was revealed when there was a dispute over setting the parish rate. The opposition was led by the non-conformist Peter Crompton and resulted in a poll. 749 voted for the proposed rate, defeating 600 who opposed it.[100]

The Chorley Poor Law Union was formed in 1837 as a consequence of the New Poor Law introduced in 1834. An Anti-Poor Law Petition was organised in Hoghton[101] and Chorley was represented at an Anti-Poor Law Meeting in Manchester[102]. However, although the minutes of the meetings of the Board of Guardians after the establishment of the Chorley Poor Law Union reflect resentment and hostility to the imposition of centralised

---

[98] *Bolton Chronicle*. 7 September 1833.
[99] "Great Conservative Dinner and Operative Procession at Chorley, Lancashire." *The Times*, 24 Nov. 1836, p.5. *The Times* Digital Archive. Accessed 18 Feb. 2019.
[100] "On Friday last a meeting of the inhabitants of Chorley was held in the parish church, for the purpose of laying a rate". *The Times*, 20 October1837, p.3. The Times Digital Archive. Accessed 6 April 2008.
[101] *Preston Chronicle* 1 April 1837.
[102] Ibid. 10 February 1838.

direction and control, there is no evidence to suggest that this was opposition of the "labouring classes."

Many working people turned to political action as the means to bring about change and, for many, this led to support for Chartists and their demands which included votes for men over the age of twenty-one, payment for MPs and a secret ballot in parliamentary elections. Chorley and Preston were represented at the Chartists' National Convention by Richard Marsden, a Preston handloom weaver. On the 5th November 1838 a great Chartist demonstration was organised in Preston attended by thousands of people. Marsden spoke on the same platform as the Chartist leader, Feargus O' Connor. One banner bore the words "No Bastilles for me- I intend to be free" and on the reverse "Sell thy garment and buy a sword."[103] He became a major national figure in the Chartist movement. Marsden spoke at meetings in Chorley and found "firm support"[104] and his constituents in Chorley and Preston wrote to him giving support for a proposed general strike in 1839.[105] Marsden attacked various vested interests in early Victorian society, including industrial capitalism;

> If food is abundant and yet its producers are famishing, must it not be obvious to everyone that the faults lie in an unjust distribution? If two classes are considered as having been equally engaged in its production, viz. the capitalist and the labourer, and if the former has more than enough and the latter too little, then it is clear that the labourer has been defrauded of his due.[106]

Violence was never far below the surface in activities at this time. In 1839 there was a rumour, reported in the *Preston Chronicle*, that local smiths were turning out pikes to arm

---

[103] Hunt, David, 1997. A History of Walton- le-Dale and Bamber Bridge. Lancaster. 145.
[104] King, J. E., 1981. Richard Marsden and the Preston Chartists 1837-1848. Lancaster. 12
[105] King. Op. Cit. 13.
[106] King. Op. Cit. 21.

Chartists[107], and the Chartists' own newspaper copied a less than sympathetic report from the *Blackburn Standard*;

> On Monday evening, as the Chartists of Chorley were discussing all the ills they would do to those opposing them in the town, a noise like the firing of cannon was suddenly heard, when a cry of "the soldiers!" was immediately raised. Out flew the Chartists, knocking down each other, whilst those behind them scampered over the prostrate bodies of their brother heroes. Many were wounded by the dirks and pikes they had with them, several receiving stabs in the part most likely to be hit in a retreating man. The noise which created such consternation was caused by blowing off a gasometer.[108]

1842 saw one of the peaks of Chartist activity, linked to the so-called Plug Riots. There was hardship and hunger across Lancashire and in Chorley there was little or no work for weavers and calico printers. In May, five hundred men paraded through the streets of Chorley seeking support.[109] They

> obtained £9 in money, upwards of 9 cwt of bread, 1 cwt of cheese and 1 cwt of bacon. On making a division, it amounted in money and goods to about 1s 2d per head.[110]

An example of working men organising themselves for their benefit.

On the 13th August the army fired on a riotous crowd in Lune Street, Preston, killing four and wounding several more. This event, and possibly a speech by Richard Marsden in Chorley, may have been the inspiration for a march of 2,000 men from Wigan to

---

[107] Heyes, Jim. Op. Cit. 114.
[108] *The Charter*. 1 September 1839.
[109] Heyes. Op. Cit. 132.
[110] *Preston Chronicle*. 17 May 1842.

Chorley. This joined a local crowd and they attacked and closed all the mills, smashing the boiler plugs. Duxbury Hall was occupied by Plug Rioters but the Yeomanry restored order and evicted them. The mob moved on through Whittle-le-Woods, Leyland, Bamber Bridge and Walton-le-Dale, armed with pikes.[111] There was a confrontation at Walton Bridge on Wednesday the 17th August, when the military fired a volley of shots and successfully turned back a large crowd of strikers from Chorley and nearby towns who had been marching on Preston in an attempt to close its mills. There were many arrests, but this time there was no bloodshed.[112]

Support for Chartism was widely based. In his study of South-East Lancashire, Robert Sykes found support not just from handloom weavers, but "by trade societies of the largest such groups of factory workers; cotton spinners, calico printers and dyers."[113]

Chartism in Chorley continued to be strongly supported. When the Great Charter was sent to London, it had 6,512 Chorley signatures. (The town's population in 1841 was 13,139). In 1846 striking powerloom weavers gathered in the town, played fife and drum and marched to formal drill.[114] In 1847, there were 128 supporters of the Chartist Land Plan in the town.[115] One of these was R. Halsale who was allocated two acres at Snigs End in June 1848. Snigs End in Gloucestershire was one of five Chartist estates established across the country. On the 21st April 1848 at least 5,000 Chartists from all over North Lancashire took part in a camp meeting at Denham Hill, Brindle, near Chorley.[116]

As Chartism evolved, it endorsed the principles of Co-operation. In 1851, The Chartist Convention, as part of its "Labour Law", declared that

---

[111] Heyes. Op. Cit. 133.
[112] King. Op. Cit. 29-30.
[113] Sykes, Robert, 1982. Early Chartism and Trade Unionism in South-East Lancashire in Edited by James Epstein and Dorothy Thompson, The Chartist Experience; Studies in Working Class Radicalism and Culture, 1830-1860. Macmillan.
[114] Heyes. Op. Cit.133.
[115] *Preston Pilot*. 20 November 1847.
[116] King. Op.Cit. 43.

> the co-operative principle is essential for the well-being of the people, since the centralization of wealth ought to be counteracted by a distributive tendency.[117]

The thousands of Chartist supporters in Chorley provided a base for the re-introduction of Co-operation in the next decade.

Another strand of working-class agitation at this time was for shorter working hours, the Ten Hours Movement. There was strong support for the campaign in Chorley. A meeting held at the Red Lion "was crowded to excess, while hundreds were unable to obtain admission."[118]

It was in this period of hardship and turmoil that the Rochdale Equitable Pioneers Co-operative Society was formed. It reflected all the working-class movements active in Rochdale in 1844.

> Half of them were Owenite Co-operators, five were Chartists, but careful piecing together of all the sources shows that at least another five were both Chartists and Co-operators.[119]

Others were involved in supporting the Ten Hours Act, Unitarianism and Teetotalism.

The story of the Rochdale Pioneers has been told on many occasions and the Co-operative movement, as part of its propaganda, has created a Rochdale mythology. It was not such a break with the past as was formerly believed, in that there had been, and still were, many successful co-operative businesses. However, what became known as the Rochdale Principles, became the template for co-operatives throughout the world. These were:-

- Democratic Control (One Man, one vote)
- Open membership

---

[117] Programme adopted by the Chartist Convention, 10 April 1851 reported in *The Christian Socialist*. 26 April 1851.
[118] "The Factory Question. Meeting at Chorley, Lancashire." *The Times*. .29 April 1844. P. 6. *The Times* Digital Archive. Accessed 6 April 2008.
[119] Birchall, Johnston. Op. Cit. 42.

- Fixed and limited interest on capital
- Distribution of the surplus as dividend on purchases
- Cash Trading
- Selling only pure and unadulterated goods
- Education
- Political and religious neutrality
- Disposal of net assets without profit to members

The rule giving one man one vote did not guarantee democracy. Where the membership was apathetic or ignorant, the organisation could be controlled by an oligarchy of a few influential people. Inevitably there were disagreements. The successful co-ops overcame those disagreements and criticisms and disruption from less committed members.

Open membership allowed new members to join after making a down payment of a shilling. They instantly shared the benefits of the other members. It encouraged the rapid growth in membership and therefore business growth.

The fixing and limiting of interest on capital was one of Robert Owen's principles. They were pragmatists, recognising that they had to attract capital to finance the business. However, being fixed, it did not rise and fall with profits. Owen's concern was that the lender should not be able to cream off the surplus made by the labour of others. The concern was to have many small investors rather than a few large ones, so that no-one could control a co-op through their personal wealth.

The distribution of surplus by the "Divi" marks a change from most earlier co-operatives where, under the Owenite influence, the aim was to build up surpluses until a co-operative community could be formed. Dividend, on the other hand, provided a more immediate benefit to those who dealt regularly with the store. It put money in the pocket of people who had previously been used to being in debt to shopkeepers. Dividend had previously been used by some co-ops in Scotland and Yorkshire. However, the Rochdale Society embedded it as a major plank of future retail co-operation. Each member had a check number and this was usually written on a check whenever a purchase was made. Triplicate copies were made; one for the customer; one for the department's records and one for the cash office. Each quarter the dividend was calculated and members could use it for further purchases or save "for a rainy day".

Cash trading was a very important principle to the Pioneers. It was recognised that a common reason for the failure of earlier societies was credit, so cash trading was adopted even though it inevitably discouraged some workers and families from membership.

The selling of unadulterated goods was not one of the original Principles but was, from the beginning, expected by members from their co-op store. They wanted a business that they could trust, which would not take advantage of them, in either quality or quantity. As described by Holyoake, in "Self Help",

> These crowds of humble working men, who never knew before when they put good food in their mouths, whose every dinner was adulterated, whose shoes let in water a month too soon, whose waistcoats shone with devil's dust, and whose wives wore calico that would not wash, now buy in the markets like millionaires, and as far as pureness of food goes, live like lords."[120]

The founders of the Chorley Pilot Industrial Co-operative Society, as will be shown later, took some of their inspiration from the Rochdale Pioneers and Holyoake's book, "Self Help."

Robert Owen had been an important educational pioneer, and Dr. King had recognised the need for the development of skills to enable co-operative businesses to be run successfully. Education activity for members and their families was to be funded by a separate levy on surpluses; this was provided through newsrooms, libraries, schools and adult education classes, managed by an Education Committee.

Political and religious neutrality was a necessary principle given the broad range of interests represented within co-operative

---

[120] Holyoake, G. J., 1857. Self Help by the People: The History of the Rochdale Pioneers. London. 1857. 39-40.

membership. Toleration of different views, opinions and beliefs was the aim, but inevitably disagreements did occur which could be disrupting and divisive.

The principle about disposal of assets was a realistic one given the failure of earlier co-operative ventures. In order to avoid attempts to break up a co-op to access the assets, in the event of a society being wound up, shareholders would be reimbursed and other assets would be distributed to other co-ops or charities.

It is important to remind ourselves that although post 1844, co-operation became identified with retailing, producer co-operatives continued to be established and run, and the retail societies also engaged in manufacturing, from clothing to food preparation, financed house building, supported the productive role of the Co-operative Wholesale Society (CWS) from 1863 and funded

> education, libraries, festivals, excursions, strikers, and in times of stress more generally, offering acceptable forms of practical assistance to the impoverished.[121]

Co-operators, including the Rochdale Pioneers, continued to follow Robert Owen's aims, particularly in respect of helping working people avoid unemployment. It was for this reason that they engaged in manufacturing, offered allotments and retained the aim of establishing self-supporting communities. Given the issues that arose in the later Chorley Pilot Industrial Co-operative Society between temperance supporters and others, it is important to note that the Rochdale Pioneers aimed at combatting the evils of drink by opening a temperance hotel.

In the next chapter I shall engage with the thorny debate as to what truly defined Co-operative Production. During the early 1850s the journal *The Christian Socialist* supported and publicised Co-operative Production ventures. A description was provided in a report to a House of Commons Committee.

---

[121] Walton, John K. Op. Cit. 115.

> In some cases several industrious men work together under regulation of their own, with a small capital, they are directed by managers whom they chose, the goods produced are sold for their common benefit, and the profits are divided among the contributors of capital and labour, in certain proportions agreed to.[122]

The *Christian Socialist* reporter J. M. F. Ludlow travelled around Lancashire and Yorkshire and his reports provide one of the main sources of information about producer and retail co-operatives at this time. As Hampson has indicated

> One of the key factors of (a producer co-operative) was that those who worked and provided labour got a share of the profits just as those who simply provided capital.[123]

The two most notable successes in Lancashire at this time were the Rochdale Co-operative Manufacturing Society, founded in 1854 by the Rochdale Pioneers, and the Padiham Commercial Company founded in 1852.

Having established a successful model in Rochdale it is generally claimed that the expansion of retail co-operation only took place after the passing of the first Industrial and Provident Societies Act in 1852 which bestowed a legal status, allowed co-operative businesses to rent and own property, and gave protection against fraud. However, a publication by the London Working Men's Association in 1852, lists over seventy co-operative societies in Lancashire, most, or all of which, will have been established before the legislation was passed and enacted.[124] Most of these were in the south eastern corner of the county, but four were in Preston. A correspondent from Preston, wrote to the LWMA that

---

[122] *Christian Socialist*. 12 April 1851.
[123] Hampson, Peter Wright, February 2015. Working Class Capitalists. The development and financing of worker-owned companies, in the Irwell Valley, 1849-1875. Unpublished Phd. Thesis. University of Central Lancashire.
[124] London Working Mens Association. Journal of Association. 1852.

the co-operative stores (four in number) are doing well; every month is extending their operations. One of the stores is negotiating for another large shop. There is also a strong desire amongs(sic) the power-loom weavers of this town to commence manufacturing on co-operative principles.[125]

Apparently "they are exclusively composed of members of the Roman Catholic persuasion."[126] A successful Store was also established in Bolton. Ludlow described it as "first-rate", with 100 members, doing £35 worth of business each week. It had been established in November 1850. In the quarter before Ludlow's visit it had paid a dividend of 1s 6d in the pound and 5% interest to shareholders.[127]

Many early retail societies were short-lived. Gurney states that about two- thirds of societies founded in 1851-2 collapsed within a decade. Successes were in the district around Manchester, and they spread north and west a few years later, especially after 1860. By 1860, the Lancashire cotton towns with parts of the West Riding of Yorkshire, already formed the heartland of co-operation.

Walton argued that the growth of co-operatives

> matched the pattern of distribution of friendly societies, trade unions and other working-class mutual assistance organisations....part of the associational and neighbourhood culture of hard work (and) thrift.[128]

At this time there is insufficient evidence in Chorley to support this view, although as will be shown, the Oddfellows were an important presence in the town, and played a major role in the founding of the Chorley Pilot Industrial Co-operative Society.

---

[125] Ibid.
[126] *Christian Socialist* Vol. ll . 1851. 167
[127] Ibid. 214.
[128] Walton. Op. Cit.118.

3

A Second Coming:
Co-operation in Chorley in the 1860s

> Upward and onward, working men,
> Our little ones shall grow
> Like olive plants beside our hearth,
> Not knowing want or woe.[129]

It is important to have a picture of Chorley in the 1850s and 1860s to better understand the development of co-operation in this period. The pattern of development, as in most towns, was uneven throughout the nineteenth century. Whilst the industrial base continued to expand, it was largely centred around processes in the textile industry, and Chorley remained the only market town in the Leyland Hundred, leaving it, arguably with one foot in industrial east Lancashire, and the other foot spread over parts of rural west Lancashire as well as the north west corner of the South Lancashire coal field.

As the industrial base grew, Chorley became more vulnerable to trade depressions. In 1838 the town had nine cotton manufacturers, employing 1800 workers.[130] The *Preston Chronicle*

---

[129] *Preston Guardian* 5 March 1862 Motto quoted by "Always a Factory Operative" in a letter to the Editor about Co-operation in Chorley.
[130] Butterworth. Op. Cit.

in 1842 described Chorley as suffering distress "probably greater than in any other town in Lancashire."[131] This distress undoubtedly helped to fuel the Chartist activities in Chorley and district described in the previous chapter.

By 1851, following the arrival of the railway in the previous decade, there were seventeen weaving, six cotton spinning and five cotton manufacturing firms in the town[132]. This would imply a doubling in textile business from 1838. It was largely as a consequence of these industrial and transport developments that the population of Chorley continued to grow. From the census figures, it can be seen that the town grew by 18.3% between 1851 and 1861. Chorley was established as the major centre of the area bordered by Bolton, Blackburn, Preston and Wigan. Firth's study of North East Lancashire showed that the growth of urban co-operative societies "closely paralleled, and was indeed largely dependent on urbanisation and industrialisation."[133]

On the other hand, the other twenty-five townships in the Chorley Union area had a mixed experience. Most declined, with only Coppull, Leyland, Withnell, Whittle-le-Woods, Adlington, Croston and Charnock Richard showing population growth. With the exception of Croston, growth in these townships would largely be associated with developments in textiles, coal or quarrying. Undoubtedly part of the growth in Chorley was fed by immigration from the surrounding townships.

Through the 1830s and 1840s and until the appointment of the Improvement Commission in the 1850s, Chorley lacked any over-arching form of local government. Instead, local magistrates, the Constable and the Board of Guardians each had their own relatively narrow areas of responsibility. Nor was there any consistent leadership from local landowners, and the leading industrial families were not sufficiently established to fill the void left by the landowning gentry, even if they wished to do so. The manor of Chorley, with its absentee lords, restricted the local market and expansion of the town. It was only in 1874 that the

---

[131] *Preston Chronicle.* 7 May 1842.
[132] Nattrass, L. B., 1974. The Governing Elite in Chorley, 1854-1914. Lancaster. Unpublished MA Dissertation.
[133] Firth. Op. Cit. 7.

Improvement Commissioners purchased the Lordship of Chorley, including the manorial rights and market place.

Arguably the one consistent leader was the Rev. J S Master, originally curate in charge of the parish church and later Rector of Chorley. Even so, that leadership would only have stretched over about a half of the population, given the substantial number of Catholics and growing Methodist and other non-conformist congregations.

The appointment of Improvement Commissioners only slowly impacted on the affairs of the town, initially in areas of sanitation, water supply and burials. They continued to use the small town hall donated to the town in 1801. (The opening of the Co-operative Hall in 1864 addressed this lack of a large public building).

Notwithstanding the founding of the Rochdale Equitable Pioneers Society in 1844, the hiatus in the development of the Co-ops lasted until legal changes were introduced by parliament which gave them a legal status and allowed them to rent and own property and gave protection against fraud. For the retail societies this legislation occurred in 1852 when the first Industrial and Provident Societies Act was passed. For other Co-operatives the key legislation came with the Limited Liability Act of 1855, and the Joint Stock Companies Act of 1856. (The Chorley Co-operative Spinning and Manufacturing Company Limited was specifically formed under the latter's regulations).

The next phase of Co-operation in Chorley, however, did not start until the beginning of the next decade. John Walton in his Social History of Lancashire describes twenty-one Lancashire Societies being founded between 1845 and 1854 and still in operation in 1912, "and for 1855-64 the figure was 67, with a spectacular peak in 1860-1." [134] These figures of course exclude those societies that had a shorter life and so the number of co-operative society foundations was much larger.

The local contribution to Walton's "spectacular peak" was made by Withnell (1861), Blackrod (1861), Bamber Bridge (1861) and Chorley Pilot Industrial Co-operative Society (1860). Other local Societies founded later in the decade were at Wheelton

---

[134] Walton Op. Cit. 245.

John E. Harrison

(1866), and Whittle-Le-Woods (1868). This was part of a wider move to found co-operatives in industrial villages and towns in weaving districts, although weaving was not the only industrial activity in these villages around Chorley. Quarrying, for example was an important industry in Withnell and Whittle-le Woods and Blackrod was part of the Wigan coal field. Timmins has shown that hand loom weaving was still an important activity in many of these communities at this time and undoubtedly was an important factor in the foundation of some of the co-operatives of this period.

John Walton describes the Rochdale model of retail co-ops as spreading rapidly in the cotton district during the 1850s. The earliest successes were in the district around Manchester, and they spread north and west a few years later, especially after 1860. Chorley and District was clearly part of the second phase, on the north west fringe of the main textile manufacturing area. However, this two-phase model of south east Lancashire followed later by north west Lancashire may need to be qualified following further local researches. In Preston and district, for example, six co-operative businesses were operating in 1851.[135] In all probability these were short-lived ventures, as in 1861 Preston was described as a place where "Co-operation is comparatively but little known."[136] However it is clear evidence of multiple co-operative ventures in central Lancashire contemporaneously with developments in Rochdale and South East Lancashire.

It is very important to remind ourselves that these were all local businesses, formed by local people, to serve specific communities. They would be small businesses, selling a few items in what Michael Winstanley described as "unprepossessing premises."[137] More than half of the twenty eight initial subscribers to the Rochdale Society were from the textile trades, the rest being "better-placed" artisans, such as shoemakers, a clogger, tailor, a joiner and a cabinet maker. They included Chartists, Owenite

---

[135] *Christian Socialist* Vol ii.201-2. 1851.
[136] Farn, J. C., April 1862. "Co-operation in Lancashire in 1861" in *The Co-operator*.
[137] Winstanley, Michael J., 1983. The Shopkeeper's World 1830-1914. Manchester.15.

Co-operators and Teetotallers. There is inevitably less detailed knowledge about a less important Society, such as Chorley's, particularly when it had a short life span.

A contemporary perspective of the Co-operative Movement in 1861 was provided by J C Farn.[138]

> Co-operation has been a long time making its way in the world. It is nearly forty years old, and yet it is only within the last forty months, or thereabouts, that it has commanded a large share of attention in the most advanced division of counties in England, to wit, South Lancashire and West Yorkshire.... Co-operation, as I understand it, is not a mere measure of hostility to shopkeepers, but a necessity which has arisen out of the circumstances of the working man. It is the bond of union for social, moral, and educational improvement, neither more nor less.... Co-operation in Rochdale is but in its infancy at the present time in the opinion of the promoters, and those who know its power.... In Bacup, we read that the profits of Co-operation have been nearly £12,000 last year; no wonder that the *"Examiner and Times"* can report that there is no increase in the poor rate on account of short time and bad trade, and append the reason,- because the working men nearly all belong to Co-operative societies; and the *"Preston Guardian"* follows up this by stating that the provident working classes of Blackburn have also done much for themselves during the past year by the same means;... In Accrington, it is reported that the poor rates are actually less than they were, and why?- because in and around that town many hundreds of working men have houses of their own, which have been erected and paid for by the agency of Co-operative societies, whole streets belonging to them;.... in Rochdale the aspect

---

[138] Farn Op. Cit.

John E. Harrison

of affairs arising from depressed trade is far more favourable than in Preston, where Co-operation is comparatively but little known. In Bury, where Co-operation thrives, no report of great distress has appeared.

Low income earners were often deterred from membership of a Co-operative Society because of the initial cost. The requirements for Accrington may well have been similar to those for the Chorley Pilot Industrial Society.

> When (attempting to join the Society) you give in your name, residence, trade or occupation, you will have to pay 1s as an entrance fee, and 4d for a copy of the rules and cash book. You will be required to make a deposit of not less than 1s towards your shares. All persons are required to take up at least 5 £1 shares and not more than 100. You can pay for your shares at once or by instalments of 1s 1d per month or 3s 3d per quarter.[139]

Farn was undoubtedly a propogandist for co-operation. However, it is interesting to note that the successes in Bury and Accrington were, like Rochdale, from small beginnings. Bury's Co-op started with £6 and Accrington's "fell well short of their target of £200".[140]

The founding of the Chorley Society was reported in the co-operative movement's newspaper *"The Co-operator"*. The report seems to have been submitted by a Chorley member:

> We had heard of the Rochdale Stores, and a poor working man purchased that useful book "Self Help". After reading it to a few friends they resolved, if possible, to open a grocery store in Chorley....the greater part refused. However, we collected our shillings together, and a few joined us weekly until we got 36 members with a capital

---

[139] *Co-operation News* 9 June 1877.
[140] Winstanley. Op Cit. 15.

of £30. We then took a shop fronting the Market Place, and forwarded our rules-which are the same as those of Manchester-to be registered.[141]

Frank Longton placed the first shop at the corner of Livesey Street and Market Place.

The book "Self Help" was probably not the more famous one by Samuel Smiles with its individualistic doctrine, but "Self Help by the People": History of Co-operation in Rochdale", by George Jacob Holyoake, which originated as a series of articles in the *Daily News*, but was published in book form in 1858. Holyoake was the most important publicist for Co-operation at this time and has been described by Johnston Birchall as an Owenite missionary. Peter Gurney has described "Self Help" as a "practical handbook for working class activists," and Holyoake as performing "an important agitational and inspirational role within the movement."[142]

Thomas Hodgkinson, the Pilot Industrial Society's Secretary, provided similar information to *"The Co-operator"*, when speaking about the founding of the Chorley Pilot Industrial Co-operative Society at the opening of the new Co-operative Hall in January 1864 (It may well have been him who provided the report to *The Co-operator* as the Secretary.):

> A few working men of this town, having heard of the benefits arising from the co-operative societies established in Rochdale and other places, met together occasionally in a cottage to discuss the propriety of establishing a society in Chorley on the Rochdale principles. A few of them went over to Rochdale to get information on the subject which was freely given, and the result was that a committee was soon formed.....A subscription of 3d per week was collected, and then they got the society enrolled according to law, and when the subscription amounted to a few pounds in the

---

[141] *The Co-operator* June 1861.
[142] Gurney, Peter, 1996. Co-operative Culture and Politics of Consumption in England 1870-1930.Manchester. 118.

> aggregate, a shop was taken and opened at nights for the first three months, the committee serving the customers in their turns and rendering their services gratis.[143]

At the end of the first quarter there were eighty-four members. Full membership was only achieved by paying in 3s 3d per quarter until £2 had been deposited in the Society.[144]

The helpfulness of the Rochdale Stores had been noted a decade earlier by Lloyd Jones, the manager of the London Co-operative Stores, after attending a Co-operative Congress in Manchester.

> It is to it (the Rochdale Stores) that nearly all new parties look for advice and direction, and the willingness with which this is given reflects great credit upon those who are engaged in the management of that establishment.[145]

Oldham was also of importance to Co-operation in Chorley. William Marcroft, the founder of the Sun Mill in Oldham spoke at a meeting in Chorley, Mr. Allen of Oldham addressed an annual meeting,[146] and William Karfoot, arguably Chorley's leading co-operator, quoted co-operative practice in Oldham.[147] It may well be that although in founding the retail society, Chorley co-operators followed guidance from Rochdale and Holyoake, in the running of that society and the Co-operative Mill, they were more influenced, for whatever reason, by practice in Oldham.

An indication of how some co-operatives started was given by a" Co-operative Tourist" and Christian Socialist, JM Ludlow on a visit to Blackburn in 1851. He did not find any co-operative store "but the germs of several, in the shape of money clubs, where a

---

[143] *Preston Guardian* 9 January 1864.
[144] *Chorley Standard* 5 October 1872.
[145] *Christian Socialist* 21 December 1850.
[146] *Chorley Standard* 17 February 1872.
[147] Ibid. 11 October 1873.

few shillings are paid in weekly for the purchase in common of provisions."[148]

A further clue as to the possible background of the founders of the Chorley Society is in the inclusion of the term "Pilot" in its title. It seems quite likely that this derived from a local lodge of Oddfellows that went under the name of "Pilot that weathered the Storm Lodge". The Lodge had been founded in 1818 by a veteran of the Peninsular War. (The phrase originated as a description of William Pitt the Younger). When the Lodge celebrated its jubilee, it was described as the first lodge established in the neighbourhood.[149] An earlier Odd Fellows-supported co-operative store had been established in Preston, "but through bad management it became seriously embarrassed, and finally closed."[150]

The poorer sections of the community could not afford to join the Oddfellows, or become Co-operative Society members or shop at the Co-operative store. At a co-operative conference in Blackburn in 1875 it was reported that "the percentage of very poor persons who are co-operators is very low indeed."[151] However Gurney emphasises that regularity of wages rather than high level was a key factor to enable a worker to become a co-operative society member.[152]

One of the leading figures in the co-operative movement in Chorley in the 1860s and 1870s, in both the mill and the retail business, was William Karfoot, and he was also a senior Oddfellow. Karfoot was for several years President of the Pilot Industrial Co-operative Society and Manager of the Co-operative Mill. He described the simple beginnings of the retail society when addressing a meeting in 1865;

> "They raised a very small capital, and commenced business in a humble way. So determined were they to be economical, that, not deeming it prudent to

---

[148] *Christian Socialist* Vol ii. 244. 1851.
[149] *Chorley Standard* 15 July 1871.
[150] *Christian Socialist* Vol. II. 167. 1851.
[151] *Co-operative News* 27 March 1875.
[152] Gurney. Op. Cit. 18.

invest any of their capital in chairs, the committee actually sat upon the floor."[153]

An alternative version of the founding of the Chorley Pilot Industrial Co-operative Society was offered in a letter to the *Preston Guardian* from "Free Trade and No Monopoly". The writer quotes a speaker at a public meeting:

> A number of men wished to begin a co-operative store, but could not raise the money. In order to get over the difficulty, they got their groceries on credit for a fortnight, as usual, at the shops where they used to trade. Now mark the scheme. When they received their wages, instead of paying the shopkeepers, they took the money (not their own) and clubbed it together, and with it started a co-operative store, or, in other words, they took the shopkeepers' money and made it a tool with which to rob him of his legitimate business.[154]

The letter resulted in four other letters to the *Preston Guardian*, three of which were from Co-operators and refuted the story. Elsewhere in his letter "Free Trade and No Monopoly" describes co-operation as an "obnoxious system" and argues that co-operative stores were not beneficial to operatives. Quite possibly the writer was a local shopkeeper and his letter illustrates that, as in other communities, co-operation in Chorley had its opponents, as well as its supporters. A trade directory of 1851 indicated that there were at least seventy-six shopkeepers, including grocers and provision dealers, before the arrival of the Co-operative Society.[155]

None the less, the new retail society was soon an integral part

---

[153] *The Co-operator* February 1865
[154] *Preston Guardian* 26 February 1862.
[155] Mannex, P. and Co., 1851.Topography and Directory of Mid Lancashire. 1851.

Co-operation in Chorley 1830-1880

of the activities of the working classes in the town. Chorley was recognised as a "Co-operative Town" in a list published in 1861.[156]

Later in 1861, a stoppage at Lightollers Mill led to workers at Smethurst's mill collecting £70 for a relief committee. Cheques for the distressed workers were drawn on the Co-operative Stores.[157]

Looking at the names of members who were mentioned in reports in the *Preston Guardian* in 1861-63, and checking them against occupations in the 1861 census and in the list of shareholder for the Co-operative Spinning and Manufacturing Company, there is clearly a strong link to the textile industry, but not just at shop-floor level as there is a cloth inspector, a book-keeper at a cotton mill, a cotton weaving manager, and two overlookers. There was also a strong teetotal faction at one time and this was the cause of some friction.

The occupational mix does seem to be somewhat similar to that of North East Lancashire where Firth states that most societies were started by weavers[158]. It will be seen from the study of village societies in the Chorley area in the Appendix that handloom weavers were important supporters of co-operation outside the growing town.

The earliest report of a quarterly meeting of the shareholders that I have found was in January 1862.[159] A dividend of 1s in the pound had been declared; receipts listed were drapery goods £130, grocery goods £2033, and the Adlington Branch store £578. The meeting was chaired by William Asting, a hand loom weaver, and the report identified the members elected to the committee. Using the census records, they were

William Asting Cotton Weaver born c 1833
William Carr Cotton Weaver born c 1838
William Aspden Calico Block Printer born c 1807
William Karfoot Cotton Weaving Manager born c 1829
Samuel Fairbrother Cotton Factory Weaver Overlooker born c1822

---

[156] *The Co-operator* August 1861
[157] *Preston Guardian* 7 December 1861.
[158] Firth op cit.
[159] *Preston Guardian* 4 January 1862.

A Whitaker (Not positively identified)
John Lewtas Cotton Weaver born 1835
Thomas Hodgkinson Secretary to Co-operative Society born 1840
Henry Whitaker Cotton Weaver born 1833

Aspden's employment as a Calico Block Printer provides the only tenuous connection between Chorley's co-operatives in the 1860s, and the earlier Owenite venture at Birkacre. He was also a shareholder in the co-operative mill, and was certainly old enough to have worked at Birkacre, but it will not be possible to prove. It is possibly more likely that he worked at Crosse Hall as that was nearer to home. Samuel Fairbrother and William Aspden, the two oldest men, were neighbours on Eaves Lane in the 1851 census. Fairbrother, as a cotton factory weaver overlooker was presumably working with power looms. Firth, in his North East Lancashire study found that power loom weaver overlookers "possessed a disproportionate influence within the co-operative movement."[160] The other committee men were largely in their twenties, and as such would have been too young to have been active Chartists, and presumably had little previous experience of running organisations.

The development of Co-operation in Chorley clearly owed much to the support and determination of its members. However, it also benefitted from the patronage and support from some of the leading figures in the town. John Rigby, Justice of the Peace and former medical practitioner became one of the main shareholders in the Co-operative Mill. His son, James Morris Rigby, also a medical practitioner, was described as President of the Co-operative Mill in 1863[161] and chaired a New Year festivities meeting in 1865 that was attended by Henry Pitman, one of the leading regional and national propagandists for co-operation. Dr. Rigby was reported as saying:

> Though he was not a member of the Society, he still felt a great interest in their welfare and success, and he felt certain that the principle of co-operation

---

[160] Firth. Op. Cit. 46.
[161] *Preston Guardian* 19 September 1863.

was calculated to encourage habits of frugality and thrift among the working classes.[162]

Dr. James M Rigby was also an Oddfellow[163], although whether he was a member of the Pilot that Weathered the Storm Lodge is not known.

Similarly, it is clear that the movement benefitted from the support of the leading factory-owning families in the town. At the tea party and soiree to celebrate the opening of the New Co-operative Hall, Major Smethurst attended, chaired the meeting and spoke in support of co-operation (The Smethursts were the leading millowner family in Chorley at this time, and important members of the Improvement Commission):

> It was the duty of every man who had got a home first of all to make it as comfortable as possible. He should mind, too, to lay out his money to the best advantage, and should be cautious, in order that he may get a fair return for it (Hear, hear.) His chief wants were good food and proper clothing; and, in order to lay out his money to advantage, he should attend establishments such as the one in connection with which they were assembled that night.[164]

Similar support was given by G H Lightoller, Cotton Spinner and John Thom, Calico Printer, in 1871 when a programme of winter lectures was initiated. Both were members of the Improvement Commission which governed Chorley.

Undoubtedly the overt support for the two new co-operative businesses of the Smethurst and Rigby families, as well as Lightoller and Thom, gave a seal of approval and respectability which encouraged membership, shareholding and custom. Firth described such support in North East Lancashire as giving "social credentials of impeccability."[165]

---

[162] *Chorley Standard* 7 January 1865.
[163] Ibid. 11 July 1868.
[164] *Preston Guardian* 9 January 1864.
[165] Firth Op. Cit.103.

John E. Harrison

The Pilot Co-op had as its motto "Our Own", and attracted 500 people to the opening of the new Co-operative Hall in 1864. It had expanded rapidly with a new bakehouse in 1863, and a branch store in Whittle le Woods in 1865, in addition to the existing Adlington branch. A further branch store in Euxton was mooted in 1865, but not proceeded with. The rapid growth in membership of urban societies as compared to village societies was described by Firth in his North East Lancashire study.[166]

The growth, coincided, somewhat surprisingly, with the Lancashire Cotton Famine. However, Chorley's economy did not rely exclusively on cotton for employment. It had collieries and a floor cloth works, two railway wagon works, and iron industries by the 1860s.

At its peak, the Chorley Pilot Society had about 1,000 members. Members would usually have been a head of household, normally male, and overall, members would have represented about 6% of the population. However, if it is assumed that there were on average four members of each co-operative society member's household, there could have been 4,000 people who benefitted in some way from the society, or 24% of the population. This is a cautious, but crude estimate and the term benefit is deliberately used to include members who shopped at the co-operative society and those who did not, but chose just to draw interest from the society.

Chorley Pilot Industrial Co-operative Society Token

---

[166] Firth Op. Cit. 7.

Co-operation in Chorley 1830-1880

The above token is one of the few pieces of evidence of the first retail Co-operative Society in Chorley. This one is held by the Chorley Heritage Group. There were several manufacturers of these tokens across the country and no evidence as to who produced this token. Some co-operatives ordered tokens from more than one supplier.

There are three main uses of Co-operative tokens. The main purpose was for dividend payment. The token had a monetary value, which varied from society to society up to £5. The value of the Chorley token is indicated as £1 on the reverse side. The use of metal tokens varied between different societies and largely died out in the early twentieth century so we cannot be totally sure how it was used in Chorley. In all probability it was given on goods sold either at the counter or at the "check" office. There would almost certainly have been tokens of lesser value or paper "checks" which would need to be exchanged for the higher value tokens before dividend would be paid on a quarterly basis.

The other uses of tokens were for showing that certain items had been pre-paid and for allowing members credit. There is no evidence to suggest how the tokens were used in Chorley. It may well have been only for dividend.

Although this society was relatively short-lived, and Frank Longton was somewhat dismissive in his description, it successfully survived the Cotton Famine and grew in terms of members and branches to be the most important retail business in Chorley. Its subsequent collapse will warrant a separate discussion.

Co-operative Production developed with support from the Christian Socialists. (The Christian Socialist Movement was a major force in the nineteenth century. Leading supporters included John Ruskin and Charles Kingsley. They saw capitalism as being rooted in greed). They, in turn had been impressed by co-operative workshops in Paris after the 1848 revolution. It was seen as a more palatable system than the capitalist system of master and servant that British industrial society was structured around.

The Chorley Co-operative Spinning and Manufacturing Company, formed one year later than the retail co-operative, was certainly an offshoot of the co-operative movement in Chorley.

Six of the retail society's 1862 committee members, listed earlier in this chapter, were also shareholders in the co-operative mill. (Messrs Asting, Aspden, W Karfoot, S Fairbrother, T Hodgkinson and H Whitaker).

However, it was not formed under the same legislation. As it needed more capital to set itself up as a manufacturing business, it sought to achieve that by being a joint stock company. Many Lancashire businesses of this period took advantage of the new legislation to attract share capital in modest amounts from local investors. Any group of seven people could form a company with limited liability, meaning that they only risked their investment. Most of these companies were not "floated" on the stock exchange as that was too expensive a process. Instead a "grey" market developed for trading these shares. Many of these new types of companies were Lancashire cotton businesses. Shares in small manufacturing business were relatively cheap at £5 or £10, but the full value was called up over a relatively short period.

These small businesses often appealed to the smaller saver as they would ask, as at the Blackburn Co-operative Cotton Spinning and Weaving Co. Ltd for example, for a deposit of 2s 6d, and calls of no more than 5s per month. In Bamford, shares were sold in a local pub on a Saturday night. In one twelve month period from the 1st July 1860 to 30 June 1861, companies with a capital of about £1.7 million were floated in the Blackburn, Bolton, Bury and Rochdale area. Many of the investors would be working men or small retailers.

Not all such companies that had "Co-operative" in their title had connections to the co-operative movement. One of the main historians of labour history, G.D.H. Cole, when writing about the proliferation of producer co-operatives in the 1860s said

> It is exceedingly difficult in this field to draw any clear lines between experiments which can be regarded as falling within the veritable field of Co-operation and other projects which, even if

Co-operation in Chorley 1830-1880

they were favoured and fostered by Co-operative leaders, were not really co-operative in essence.[167]

More recently, with hindsight, Chesters has suggested a three-part test to assess whether a business was truly "co-operative"[168]:

- Investment by the working class by loans or shares.
- Employee control and all employees were members of the company.
- Profits were divided between capital and labour.

There is no doubt that for many years, the national co-operative movement struggled at its annual meetings with the definition of "producer co-operative". For example, at the Fifth Annual Congress held in Newcastle in April 1873 there was extensive debate around resolutions defining what kind of society should be recognised as a co-operative society.

> All productive societies or companies which provide in their rules for a just and equitable division of all nett profits between capital, labour and, as far as practicable, trade.[169]

Many views were expressed and no firm decision on a definition was taken. One of the more interesting views was expressed by William Marcroft of Oldham.

> He thought that co-operative societies were yet in their infancy, and that they could hardly yet say how a co-operative society should be defined. He did not want a hard and fast line laid down that might hereafter be inconvenient.

---

[167] Cole, G.D.H., 1944. A Century of Co-operation. London.158.
[168] Chesters, Alan, 2006. "Working Class Limiteds: Co-operative Cotton Companies in S. E. Lancashire, 1850-1880. Unpublished MA Dissertation Lancaster.33.
[169] Fifth Annual Co-operative Congress. Published Manchester 1873.

John E. Harrison

Marcroft was the only co-operator from outside of Chorley who I have found mentioned in connection with the Chorley Mill. He addressed a Tea Party held on behalf of the mill in 1867[170] and advocated the adoption of loans to the company, a system that he had used at the Sun Mill at Chadderton.

The Sun Mill was Oldham's first Co-operative Mill. "Having obtained the initial capital for the mill by 1862, shareholders were then offered employment at the company."[171] Oldham "Limiteds" were important joint-stock manufacturing businesses. It was a

> system of capitalism founded on principles of democracy, where share -ownership conferred the rights and obligations of participation in the management of companies by the shareholders themselves, many of whom were mill-operatives.[172]

Given the dates of the foundation of the Chorley and Oldham mills it is unlikely that one followed the other, but it illustrates a breadth of vision amongst promoters of textile businesses founded for textile workers. It may well be that the directors and shareholders of the Chorley Co-operative Mill saw themselves as going along the same road as the Sun Mill and other "Oldham Limiteds".

In the retail sector, Rochdale was the template and most subsequent societies followed that model. No such template existed in the 1860s for co-operators in Chorley seeking to establish their own cotton mill. It was only in the next decade that the Hebden Bridge Fustian Manufacturing Society was formed, and that became a model as a successful producer co-operative.

The *Preston Guardian* reported

> On Tuesday last at a numerous meeting at the Curriers Arms Inn, Chorley, it was resolved to establish a spinning and weaving company on

---

[170] *Chorley Standard*. 29 June 1867.
[171] Toms, S., 2007. <u>Oldham Capitalism and the Rise of the Lancashire Textile Industry.</u> Working Paper number 30. 6. University of York.
[172] Toms. Op. Cit. 3.

co-operative principles, in Chorley. It is proposed to raise £20,000 in shares of small amounts.[173]

By January 1862, when the company submitted the first of its annual lists of shareholders, the nominal capital of the company was £20,000 divided up into 20,000 shares of £1 each, payable in twenty monthly calls of a shilling each. At that time 3788 shares had been taken up. There had been eight monthly calls of a shilling and £1,584 11s had been received. This was clearly a long way short of the proposed £20,000. However, it was sufficient to fund the lease of a large piece of land off Steeley Lane for 999 years. When the Company was liquidated, the land was described as being 20,893 square yards, of which two thirds were undeveloped. This is perhaps testimony to the ambition of the founders, but perhaps indicates that as Co-operators they hoped to build more than a weaving shed. As it was, they only built eight houses on Steeley Lane, numbered 41-55.

By April 1862 the mill was under construction, and by 1863 the Improvement Commissioners' Valuation list shows a weaving shed on Steeley Lane belonging to the Co-operative Company with a rateable value of £145. This appeared to be mid-range in terms of mill rateable values in Chorley, as Barton's at Crosse Hall was £220 and Saville's in Bolton Street was £99.

That notwithstanding, the company required more capital and in 1863 decided "that the present shares be made into £10 shares in lieu of £1 shares, and that Half Shares be allowed to be taken up". Presumably they were not hopeful of widening the range of investors and therefore sought to raise more from the existing investors. This was of course in the midst of the Cotton Famine! By June 1868, 599 shares had been fully called up, giving capital of just under £6,000.

Who were these shareholders? Some are names that are known through involvement with the Chorley Pilot Industrial Co-operative Society. At a tea party in 1866, John Windsor (Power-loom weaver of Crosse Hall), who was not one of the directors, claimed that it was he along with two others who had first

---

[173] *Preston Guardian* 2 March 1861.

John E. Harrison

"mooted the erection of a co-operative shed." (In the following year Windsor chaired a meeting in Chorley in support of the Eight Hours Movement.) William Asting (Hand Loom Weaver) declared that he was one of the others.[174]

From the 1862 list of shareholders we have 167 names, one of which was a male and female joint shareholding, possibly man and wife. Twenty-nine of the shareholders were women, almost a fifth. This figure is not dissimilar to the figure of 14% that Peter Hampson arrived at when analysing shareholders of twenty three companies in the Irwell Valley in the period 1849-75.[175] Hampson's research showed that many of the women "were essentially mill girls, ie textile operatives who mostly gave their occupations as power loom weavers."[176] Twelve of the twenty nine women who were shareholders in the Chorley Co-operative Mill in 1862, listed their occupation as power loom weaver.

This involvement of "mill girls" should not be a surprise. Women outnumbered men in the textile industries' workforce. Women who were spinsters or widows and working in the mills were independent earners,[177] and women who were power loom weavers were paid at piecework rate, the same as men.[178] Hampson concluded "that working class women in the period in question had money to spare and the ability and freedom to decide how to utilise it."[179]

The majority of the shareholders in the Chorley Co-operative Mill lived within Chorley. Of the forty-five who lived outside, the vast majority lived in neighbouring communities such as Heapey, Whittle le Woods and Wheelton. There were single shareholders in Blackburn and Preston and three in Bolton.

The addresses of the Chorley shareholders were scattered across the town, but the two most frequently mentioned streets

---

[174] *Chorley Standard* 3 November 1866
[175] Hampson. Op. Cit. 143.
[176] Hampson. Op. Cit. 131
[177] Thompson, E.P., 1970. <u>The Making of the English Working Class</u>. London.452.
[178] Morgan, Carole E., January 1992. "Work and Consciousness in the Mid-Nineteenth-Century English Cotton Industry" in Social History, Vol 17, No1.31.
[179] Hampson. Op. Cit. 143.

were on the east side of the town close to the site of the mill. These were Lyons Lane and Eaves Lane with twenty and twenty-one shareholders respectively. Hampson's research in the Irwell Valley found that buying of shares "was often alongside their neighbours, relatives or workmates" with "probably quite a lot of peer pressure, as well as an element of keeping up with the Joneses."[180]

Unsurprisingly, most of the shareholders (98/167) had occupations associated with textiles, be it in preparation, spinning, weaving or finishing. The largest group, however, was that of power loom weavers (37/98). It is not known where they worked, but it is probable that many, if not most, worked at the Co-op mill. As well as shop floor workers, there were also shareholders from the supervisory level; five overlookers and two cloth inspectors.

Those shareholders from a non-textile background were thinly spread across a range of occupations from innkeeper, sexton, butler, surgeon, veterinary surgeon, and collier to farmers (Four). Many of the largest shareholders were drawn from this non-textile group. The largest shareholder, with £200 of shares was George Livesey, a veterinary surgeon. There were fourteen shareholders with holdings of £100 or more, and they and their families and households held £1590, or 42% of the total share capital. The Articles of Association allowed a vote to those shareholders holding five or more shares. In 1862, only seventeen shareholders were unable to vote. However, as a result of increasing the value of shares from £1 to £10, 118 shareholders were unable to vote, and therefore control was far more concentrated. There is no evidence to indicate that this was the primary aim of increasing the value of the shares. It was almost certainly designed to raise additional capital for the company.

Information about dividend payments to shareholders is sparse. However, William Karfoot claimed in 1869 "that every shareholder up to the present had received five per cent upon their money, except in one year."[181]

This pattern of shareholding had not changed significantly

---

[180] Hampson. Op. Cit. 180 - 182.
[181] *Chorley Standard* 20 March 1869.

in the only other surviving shareholders list in 1867. However, there was a change in the leading personalities. George Livesey had twenty-three £10 shares, but the leading shareholder was John Rigby, Justice of the Peace and a retired general medical practitioner, followed by William Karfoot with thirty-three and a half shares. His brother, Mathias, a cashier, held nineteen shares. It was the Karfoots, and particularly William, who were the leading figures in Co-operation in Chorley through the 1860s and 1870s.

The initial list of Directors was included in the Memorandum and Articles of Association.

- George Livesey; Veterinary Surgeon. Subscribed 100 shares in the Memorandum, but actually bought 200. This converted to twenty in 1867. 6 March 1861 he was described as the Treasurer.
- John Pollard; Surgeon. 100 shares. Eleven shares in 1867. Invalid from 1871. Died in 1878. 6 March 1861 he chaired a meeting of shareholders.
- Richard Barton; Agent (1861), Accountant (1867). 100 shares. Sixteen shares in 1867. 1871 House Agent. Chairman 1872/3.
- James Longworth; Block Printer. Fifty shares. Two in 1867.
- William Leach; Overlooker. Fifty shares.
- Henry Whittaker; Power Loom Weaver (1861), Innkeeper (1867). Fifty shares. Five in 1867. 1871 Licensed victualler.
- John Windsor; Power Loom Weaver. Twenty-five shares. Four in 1867.
- John Holden; Power Loom Weaver. Twenty shares.
- Henry Croston; Innkeeper. Twenty shares. Two in 1867. 1866 meeting at held at the Cunliffe Arms which was his public house.
- Joseph Gillibrand: 1873 retiring director, but re-elected. 1862 ten shares. 1867 Overlooker. Three shares.
- Robert Jolly: 1873 retiring director, but re-elected. 1867 Engineer Seven shares.
- Josiah Taylor. 1873 retiring director, but re-elected. 1867 Carder Eighteen shares.

On the basis of what is known, the Chorley business does not pass the three- part test suggested by Chesters to prove whether the business was truly a co-operative producer. Although most of the investors in the business were "working class", and in all probability many of the employees were shareholders, there is no evidence that all employees were members of the company. Similarly, there is no evidence of employee control and rather the suspicion that control lay with the larger shareholders, who were mainly not likely to be employees, or even working class. The final test was with the division of profits between capital and labour. Again, there is no real evidence, but it would appear that employees only received their wages, unless if they were also shareholders, they would also be paid dividend on their shares. It was the issue of "bonus to labour" which eventually would be the crucial test to define true producer co-operatives. Employees would be entitled to a share of the profits, as would investors and customers. This issue caused severe schisms in the national co-operative movement, particularly as the Co-op's Wholesale arm, the CWS, as it moved into production, did not give a "bonus to labour", but only paid wages to its employees.

It would be rash to dismiss the Chorley business as not being truly co-operative. I would argue that the Chorley Co-operative Spinning and Manufacturing Company aimed at being "co-operative." This was a period of experimentation, with no clear template for producer co-operatives to follow. There were clearly connections between the retail and producer co-operatives in Chorley at this time; there was an overlap of personnel, all of whom would be described as co-operators. In later years the relationship between employees and managers was sometimes difficult and managers and directors were accused by employees and unions of not acting in the spirit of co-operation. They saw it as a co-operative business that at times was not true to the principles of co-operation, and that is a view that I share.

4

William Karfoot: A Chorley Co-operator and more

Gurney has stated that most leading local and national co-operators were non-conformists[182]. The largest denominations were Methodists and Congregationalists. It is not possible as yet to state whether or not all the leading Chorley co-operators fit this picture. However, William Karfoot and his brother Mathias were both baptised at Hollinshead Street Independent Chapel in Chorley, in 1828 and 1823 respectively. They and their families were important members of this Chapel throughout their lives. A report in 1870 refers to them both giving recitations at the Hollinshead Street Sunday School Annual Christmas Tea Party[183]. One, at least, of the Karfoots was also involved with the British and Foreign Bible Society.[184] As a product of his faith and support for Co-operation, William was involved in supporting the Temperance Movement. He addressed a Temperance Tea Party in 1866.[185](Divisions between Temperance supporters and their opponents became an issue in the Chorley Pilot Industrial Co-operative Society).

Their father, another William, was a handloom weaver from Ulnes Walton, between Chorley and Croston. The family name

---

[182] Gurney, Peter. Op. Cit. 48.
[183] *Chorley Standard* 31 December 1870.
[184] *Preston Guardian* 18 September 1869.
[185] *Chorley Standard* 3 November 1866.

was almost always spelt with an "a", although Kerfoot is the more common spelling in Chorley. Interestingly Ralph Kerfoot from Chowbent, near Atherton (a former Luddite stronghold), was a well-known Chartist who emigrated to Rouen in 1839 and later supported the Chartist Land Plan.

Mathias was described as a cotton warehouseman in the 1841 census, but by 1851 he was a book keeper, and it was these skills that he brought to the Co-operative movement in Chorley, particularly as the long-term auditor to the retail co-operative. The younger William was described as a warper in the 1851 census. The Karfoots lived on Preston Street and worked in the near-by mills owned by the Smethurst family.

Co-operation became a major theme in the lives of the Karfoots, but they were to remain active across a wide range of interests and issues across the town. In 1856 both brothers attended the dinner for 220 people which celebrated the Treaty of Paris and the end of the Crimean War. [186]Both were involved with the Chorley Permanent Building Society; Mathias was listed as a committee member of the new society in 1859[187], and William was an auditor in 1861[188].

William continued to be employed by the mill-owning Smethursts, rising to become an overlooker and in 1866 he attended the wedding of Augustus Smethurst's daughter, and made a speech and toast, referring to "their worthy master"[189]

There was an important political dimension to the Karfoots. Like the Smethursts, they were Liberals, and in 1861 *The Co-operator* noted that it was a feature of early leading co-operators for them to be active in the Liberal Party.[190] Firth found that in in his study that Liberal politicians were involved in the running of local societies and occupied management roles.[191]

In 1866, it was clear that both brothers were leading Chorley figures in the campaign to widen the franchise. Both were on the

---

[186] *Preston Guardian* 31 May 1856.
[187] Ibid. 26 February 1859.
[188] Ibid. 9 March 1861.
[189] *Chorley Standard* 9 June 1866
[190] *The Co-operator* 1861-2 p83.
[191] Firth. Op. Cit. 76.

Co-operation in Chorley 1830-1880

platform of a public meeting chaired by the mill owner William Lawrence. William Karfoot presented a resolution that he had been given and in supporting it he said

> when the working man, who has been the sinew and bone of this country, who has been the very means of accumulating those riches, with all our large boast of honour, I ask "how are the taxes to be spent that I help to pay?" Can I vote who shall be my representative in parliament or who we shall send to Parliament to represent us as a borough? The answer is "Now we will trust you with bayonets, we will trust you with swords, we will trust you with anything but the power of voting, we want to reserve that to ourselves.[192]

Later in the year William Karfoot was elected to the Reform Union Committee[193], and in 1873 William moved the resolution to establish a Liberal Reform Club, to be known as the Chorley United Reform Club. Both brothers were on the committee.[194] This marked a step forward in organised political parties in Chorley and William's name came to be seen on nominations of "Liberals" to seek election to the Chorley Improvement Commission.

William was also a supporter of the ideas of Richard Cobden, one-time Chorley Millowner and Anti-Corn Law League campaigner. He offered the vote of thanks at a lecture given about Cobden in Chorley in 1870. "He expressed a hope that we should have many more such men as Richard Cobden."[195] In some parts of Lancashire Cobden and his colleague John Bright were remembered more for their opposition to the Factory Acts.[196]

The Karfoot brothers' campaigning did not end with the franchise. Like many non-conformists they resented the power and influence of the Church of England. In 1872 William chaired

---

[192] *Chorley Standard* 29 September 1866.
[193] Ibid. 10 November 1866,
[194] Ibid. 24 May 1873.
[195] Ibid. 4 June 1870.
[196] Marshall, J. D., 1974. Lancashire. Newton Abbot. 86.

John E. Harrison

a meeting on the disestablishment of the Church of England. The platform included local ministers, his brother Mathias and the mill owner, William Lawrence.[197] The local power of the Vestry had diminished significantly as the century progressed, but it was clearly still of some importance as both brothers attended the annual Easter meeting in 1877.[198]

William's involvement with Co-operation almost certainly came through his connections with Friendly Societies, and particularly the Oddfellows, and it was the Pilot that Weathered the Storm Lodge of Oddfellows that played a leading role in establishing the Chorley Pilot Industrial Co-operative Society. In 1861 a Mr. Karfoot (probably William) spoke at the celebrations for the opening of a new lodge of the Manchester Unity of Oddfellows. He said

> that this, and other societies of a similar nature, were the very thing that would remove pauperism from the country, for the working classes were becoming more independent.[199]

Co-operation was a natural progression for members of Friendly Societies and its importance was expressed in a motion that William Karfoot moved at a retail co-operative meeting in 1866:

> This meeting is of the opinion that the Co-operative Movement is calculated to promote the best interests of the working classes, by inculcating a desire for self-help, and for that reason, it is heartily recommended to the attention of all working-men who are desirous of bettering their social position.[200]

---

[197] *Chorley Standard* 7 December 1872.
[198] Ibid. 31 March 1877.
[199] *Preston Guardian* 24 August 1861.
[200] *Chorley Standard* 8 December 1866.

Co-operation in Chorley 1830-1880

William was reported as being elected to the retail society's committee in January 1862,[201] and was first reported to chair a quarterly meeting of members the following year.[202] He almost certainly chaired more such meetings over the following seventeen years than any other member. His brother Mathias was appointed one of the auditors in 1863 and he seems to have carried out this function through most of the same period.

As leading members in the retail society they spoke on occasions other than the quarterly meetings. For example, in 1864, both spoke at a meeting convened to promote the idea of building a Co-operative Hall. The meeting was initially chaired by Major Smethurst, but William took over.[203]

Although both became shareholders, their first reported connection with the Co-operative Mill was when they both spoke at a Tea Party which, whilst celebrating the installation of mill machinery, was presumably being held to promote shareholding in the mill.[204]

---

[201] *Preston Guardian* 4 January 1862.
[202] Ibid. 4 April 1863.
[203] Ibid. 9 January 1864.
[204] *Preston Chronicle*, 19 Sept. 1863. *British Library Newspapers,* https://link.gale.com/apps/doc/Y3207462361/BNCN?u=lancs&sid=BNCN&xid=aaea5f49. Accessed 15 Jan. 2020.

John E. Harrison

> spacious shed and two waiting rooms, with excellent and ample platform accommodation on both sides. There still exists, however, close to the station, the dangerous nuisance of a much frequented crossing, although it will probably not be attended with quite so much danger as formerly.
>
> CHORLEY CO-OPERATIVE TEA PARTY.—On Saturday, a tea meeting was held in the new weaving shed belonging to the Chorley Co-operative Spinning and Weaving Company (Limited), the occasion being the completion of the engine, shafting, and other works. About 150 shareholders and their friends sat down to the repast, which included roast beef and sandwiches. The company being all in the best apparent humour, the edibles speedily disappeared. The tables were cleared, and, in the absence of the president, Mr. J. M. Rigby, M.D., Mr. Josiah Taylor was called to the chair, and in a humorous but effective speech, he recounted some of the difficulties with which the company had had to contend since their commencement, and the manner in which, by dint of persevering energy, they had been overcome. Now that the engine, shafting, &c., were complete, they were assembled, and might be said to be enjoying themselves, on their own premises. The meeting was further addressed by Messrs. M. and W. Karfoot, H. Croston, H. Nightingale, and others, all of whom congratulated the shareholders upon the success of the undertaking, and urged upon those present to inform their relatives and friends that, as a limited number of shares in their present form might still be had, of the importance of availing themselves of the opportunity thus afforded them of pushing their way in the world. The engine, we understand, is a highly-finished horizontal one, and made by Mr. Hugh Heald, of Chorley. The weaving shed will at present afford space for 300 looms, and arrangements have been made for extensions, so that it may hold 800 looms. Arrangements have likewise been made for carrying on a spinning department as soon as it is found desirable. The usual votes of thanks were accorded to the chairman and to the ladies, and a cordial vote of confidence was likewise passed to the company's directors, after which the young people engaged in the merry dance, which was kept up with spirit until eleven o'clock, when the proceedings closed with the National Anthem.
>
> BOARD OF GUARDIANS.—The weekly meeting of this board was held on Tuesday last, when the books showed the number of paupers in receipt of relief to be,—In-door, Chorley district, 86; Brindle, 91 — Out-door, Chorley, 889; Leyland, 1,515; Croston, 447. The masters' books showed the amounts received into the houses to be—Chorley, £16 11s. 11d.; produce of

Cutting from the Preston Guardian 19 September 1863

The frequency with which William Karfoot is mentioned as speaking at a wide range of meetings would seem to indicate that he was a confident and capable orator who was not intimidated by being on the same platform as local millowners or national figures from the co-operative movement. An example of the latter occurred at the New Year festivities held at the Co-operative Hall in 1865, when the main speaker was Henry Pitman, editor of

"The Co-operator". William Karfoot was described as addressing the meeting "in a very able manner."[205]

William seems to have usually erred on the side of caution in developing co-operation in Chorley. This is evidenced for example in the development of the "Education Department", Reading room and library as will be seen in a later chapter. However, there is no doubt that he was committed to advancing the rights of the working man, be he employed by the Co-op or elsewhere. In 1868 he supported a half day holiday for employees of the retail society "at the same wages". He considered "as a body of working men (they should) set a good example." He compared it to the Ten Hours bill- the same work could be done in ten as in twelve hours and be better paid. Workers would return with "renewed energy."[206]

Neither of the brothers appeared in the 1862 listing of shareholders of the Co-operative Mill. However, the Margaret Kerfoot, housekeeper of Lyons Lane who had five shares could well be Mathias's wife and the William Kerfoot, school boy of Lyons Lane could well be their son. A further William Kerfoot, a gardener of Whittle-le- Woods was listed as holding 100 shares. He may have been related to the Karfoot brothers. As William, at least, was still working for a millowner in the town, it may well have been felt prudent to hide their initial investment in the Co-operative Mill. However, they were in the 1867 listing of shareholders, William holding thirty-three and a half and Mathias nineteen of the £10 shares. As such they were two of the more significant shareholders in Chorley's Co-operative Mill.

In the short life of both the retail co-operative and the Co-operative Mill, the Karfoots quickly achieved the status of being leading Co-operators in the town. When a delegation of three leading co-operators went to negotiate with Mr. Rigby over the purchase of land, one was inevitably a Karfoot (actual brother not named).[207] Mathias addressed a tea party in Adlington[208] and supported the retail co-op's expansion into Whittle-le-Woods.[209]

---

[205] *Chorley Standard* 7 January 1865.
[206] Ibid. 10 October 1868
[207] *Preston Guardian* 9 April 1864.
[208] *Chorley Standard* 4 November 1865.
[209] Ibid. 19 August 1865.

John E. Harrison

In 1869, William Karfoot was reported to have addressed meetings of the Wheelton Prospect Industrial Co-operative Society and the Whittle-le Woods Star Co-operative Society. This form of "missionary" work was common throughout the co-operative movement and William's invitations may well have reflected his perceived importance in the local co-operative community as well as his skill in public speaking. William was described as an "accomplished story teller." It may well also have been a part of a "reaching out exercise" by the Chorley Society as Thomas Hodgkinson, the Society's secretary was also involved in the Whittle meeting.

Tea Parties were popular events which served to help to bond together the community of co-operative members, advertise the success of co-operative businesses and promote the temperance message espoused by many leading co-operators. For several years the Chorley Pilot Industrial Co-operative Society held an annual tea party and the Karfoot brothers often featured as speakers as in the one in 1866, described below[210]:

> **CHORLEY.**
> TEA MEETING.—The sixth annual tea meeting in connection with the co-operative society, was held on Saturday last, in the Co-operative Hall, when about 180 persons sat down to tea, after which addresses on co-operation were delivered by Messrs. J. Perkins, of Heath Charnock; T. Slater, of Bury; W. Karfoot, M. Karfoot, and J. Critchley, of Chorley. The latter part of the evening was spent in dancing, and other amusements. The report which was read showed the society to be in a very prosperous state.
>
> LECTURES.—On Monday evening a lecture was delivered in the Co-operative Hall, under the auspices of the United

Tea Meeting Preston Guardian 8 December 1866

There is a sense in the various reports over almost two decades that William Karfoot, in the senior role that he plays

---

[210] *Preston Chronicle*, 8 Dec. 1866. *British Library Newspapers*, https://link.gale.com/apps/doc/Y3207469016/BNCN?u=lancs&sid=BNCN&xid=2158042d. Accessed 15 Jan. 2020.

in the local co-operative movement, becomes more distanced from the ordinary membership. That is seen in particular with the affairs of the Co-operative Mill and seemed to start in 1867 with a dispute between the managers of the Mill and the Union.[211] William Karfoot was presumably a member of the Co-operative Mill's management at that time and wrote to the local paper justifying their stance. This was publicly challenged by the trade union secretary in his own letter to the Chorley Standard.

It was towards the end of the 1860s that newspaper reports of the quarterly meetings began to provide evidence that all was not always well with the retail society and disagreements arose. On one occasion William Karfoot, the Chairman, was reported as having an acrimonious discussion with a member about changes in the running of the business and the impact on the dividend.[212]

In 1869 William Karfoot left the shop floor to become a manager. He had worked for the Smethursts for nine years and had been an overlooker. He moved to the Co-operative Mill as its manager. A presentation evening was held at the Co-operative Hall to mark his departure from Smethursts.[213] Within four years William became Secretary, pro tem, of the local textile employers' Association.[214]

In 1875 William Karfoot again found himself in a dispute with the Weavers' Union. There was a dispute about payments and a strike was threatened. Mr. Birtwistle, the Union general secretary argued that "If they (percentages) were put on in the way proposed by Mr. Karfoot, the weavers would suffer a considerable reduction in wages." Others argued that Co-operation was "never intended for the pulling down of wages."[215]

William continued to Chair the quarterly meetings of the retail society. There is nothing in the reports to indicate that he was viewed differently because of his role as an employer. However, it would have been natural for the acrimony to have spread to the affairs of the retail society, particularly as that

---

[211] *Chorley Standard* 5 October 1867.
[212] Ibid. 9 January 1869.
[213] Ibid. 13 March 1869.
[214] Ibid. 17 May 1873.
[215] Ibid. 26 June 1875.

society had started to struggle and there were an increasing number of issues to challenge the Management Committee about. Chairing such meetings became more difficult. On one occasion in 1876 the newspaper gave a line by line account of an argument between Karfoot and one of the members. In the preamble to the report, the meeting was described as "lively."[216] It appeared that William stopped chairing meetings from 1877, although he continued on the Management Committee. He must have continued as the leading figure at the Co-operative Mill, as in early 1879, along with Mr. Smethurst he led the employers' side in another dispute with mill workers. Later in May 1879, he was one of the petitioners for the winding up of the Mill business. He was still described as Mill Manager.

William and Mathias Karfoot saw both of Chorley's co-operative businesses grow and fail. They stayed involved throughout; Mathias in his role as auditor with the retail society, and one of the petitioners for the winding up of the Co-operative Mill. William, because of his management role at the Co-op Mill and as a senior figure in the retail movement, seemed to have become more detached from the life of the ordinary co-operative supporter. Neither seem to have played any role in the last few months of the retail society.

---

[216] Ibid. 27 May 1876.

5

The Chorley Co-operative Spinning and Manufacturing Company

The Co-operative Mill never achieved the £20,000 capital that was its original target, and that meant that it never achieved the size and breadth of business that was originally aimed for. Its business and trading experience during the years of its operation were not dissimilar to those of other Lancashire textile businesses of the same size. A flavour of the members' pride can be found in the following report from a tea party held in 1866 to celebrate an extension to the mill. In particular note the caution of one of the directors. (The mill was often referred to as Greenfield Mill).

> On Saturday evening the work people at the Greenfield Spinning and Manufacturing Company's mill, and a few others, to the number of about 70, had a social tea party at the Co-operative Hall, at the expense of the manager, directors and others. A substantial repast was served by the Co-operative Society, and being flavoured with a drop of the "crater"(?), hilarity was the order of the day. One of the shareholders afterwards presided, and made some suitable remarks upon co-operation. Mr. John

Windsor proposed the health of the "Directors", and said that he had known them sufficiently long to have confidence in them. He believed that at the Greenfield shed the workpeople could get as much or more money for weaving than they could get at many places. A weaver with three looms could earn better than a pound a week, and he thought that they could not do better than that anywhere else. He adverted to some little difficulty there had been between the workpeople and the directors recently, but that, he believed, had been cleared up satisfactorily both to the weavers and the directors. He (Mr. Windsor), along with two others, was the first who mooted the erection of a co-operative shed, and since that time he had always been connected with it, and had never had his confidence in it shaken. From the way in which it was carried on, he believed it would succeed. Whenever the weavers were getting good money, there was sure to be a large dividend for the shareholders.[217]

It seems that the business was never able to sell more than the 599.9 £10 shares that were recorded in the 1867 list of shareholders. Other options were explored. In 1867, William Marcroft, another Co-operator, from the Sun Mill, Chadderton, near Oldham, addressed a special meeting on the benefits of obtaining loans from "persons desirous of investing". It was hoped that loans receiving 5% interest would be attracted from working men and from friendly societies with surplus money.[218]

The Oldham connection is important because as a town it had a "progressive brand of democratic and stock market-based capitalism"[219]. Textile businesses known as "Oldham Limiteds" were

---

[217] *Chorley Standard* 3 November 1866
[218] Ibid. 29 June 1867.
[219] Toms. 3.

a unique phenomenon in economic history...a system of capitalism based on democracy, where share ownership conferred the rights and obligations of participation in the management of companies by the shareholders themselves, many of whom were mill operatives.

Loan stock was popular in the "Oldham Limiteds" as "local people could use the company as a type of bank, depositing money and receiving interest."[220] Money was also more readily available, usually at a month's notice. At the same time this enabled shareholders in successful companies to draw a better dividend.

The Co-operative Mill advertised for loans shortly after Marcroft's speech.

> Notice to Shareholders and Others. Opening of a Loan Account. The directors of this company have great pleasure in informing the Public that in compliance with the request of several Shareholders and others, they are now prepared to receive loans from parties wishing to invest. Loan deposits will be received at the Company's office, Greenfield Mill, on Mondays and Thursdays from 9am to 4pm. Interest at the rate of 5 per cent per annum will be paid on all complete pounds, from the date of deposit to the date of withdrawal. Scale of notices for withdrawal of loans:- £5 on application, £10 one week, £20 two weeks, £40 three weeks, £60 four weeks, £80 five weeks, £100 six weeks, sums above £100 eight weeks. Payment of interest on loans will be half-yearly, and if not withdrawn at the appointed time will be entered as a Loan at Interest. Parties who have money at their disposal will find in this a rare opportunity of investing it, as it supplies a want which has

---

[220] Hampson. Op. Cit. 174.

> long been felt in the neighbourhood. R. Richardson
> Secretary. [221]

I have not found any further information about the loans, but I assume that the sums raised did not make a significant difference to the fortunes of the Co-operative Mill.

In Chapter 3, I referred to the debates over the years about definitions of co-operative production. Marcroft was a significant contributor to that debate. He certainly saw himself as a co-operator and was recognised by others as such, not only because of his role in co-operation in Oldham and Chadderton, but also because he helped to promote the Co-operative Insurance Society and was a vigorous advocate of the Co-operative Wholesale Society. More recently, he has been recognised as the "high priest of industrial co-operation."[222]

The week after Marcroft's visit there was a fractious discussion at the retail society about the possibility of some of its surplus capital being invested in the Co-operative Mill. William Karfoot, on behalf of the mill

> denied the matter most emphatically, and forcibly told them the Spinning Company did not require their money, but he would state that the Spinning Company were safer in point of security than the Stores. [223]

Karfoot's comment fuelled a heated debate which illustrated disagreements between members of the retail and manufacturing societies.

> Mr. W. Karfoot made a remark to the effect that he had been told that a director of the Stores had endeavoured to damage the reputation of the Spinning Mill by some expressions he had used to certain cotton masters with whom they had been

---

[221] *Chorley Standard* 3 August 1867.
[222] Toms. Op. Cit. 4.
[223] *Chorley Standard* 6 July 1867

> trading. This at once caused Mr. Moore, one of the committee, to jump up and demand Mr. Karfoot's informant; Mr. Carr at the same time remarking that the "cap seemed to fit". Loud talk and banter then grew apace, and the chairman came in for a sound lecture upon his "uncharitableness" and injudiciousness in making such remarks.- Mr. Karfoot at length gave the name of his informant, when it appeared that the gentleman who "felt the sting", and whom the "cap seemed to fit", had somehow or other got confounded in the persons and had to return quietly to his shell. The warmth of the meeting, however, continued for some time.[224]

No financial help was given by the retail society, but clearly co-operators were casting around for a means of addressing the capital shortfall at the mill. For the Co-operative Mill, with hindsight, this was a missed opportunity. The retail society was as yet in a strong financial position and was certainly in a situation where it could have provided additional capital. In the following decade, "significant" amounts of loan and equity capital were provided to the "Oldham Limiteds" by local retail co-operatives.[225]

Later in 1867 the Co-operative Mill found itself in dispute with its workers, and this dispute showed that co-operators were seeing the two co-operative businesses in different lights. The details of the dispute around the payments for yarns of different descriptions are not important. The weavers were on strike for several weeks and were represented by the General Secretary of their union, Thomas Birtwistle. At a meeting of 200 weavers held in Chorley's Co-operative Hall:

> The Chairman (Mr. Carr) also remarked that an impression existed that the Co-operative Spinning Company and the Pilot Industrial Stores were

---

[224] Ibid.
[225] Toms. Op. Cit. 9.

identical societies, but he wished to dispense that impression- there was no identity between them whatever. He was one who had something to do with the origination of the Co-operative Spinning Company, but little did they think that the company was not existing upon the principle of co-operative societies, namely giving profits to labour. Capital was nothing without labour, hence it was that labour was recognised in the establishment of co-operatives generally, but it was not so at the co-operative spinning mill - they had nothing there except trying to lower the scale of labour by lowering wages.[226]

It clearly failed the "bonus to labour" test. (William Carr was a weaver and one of the founders of the Pilot Industrial Stores.)

It appears that although he was not yet the manager at the mill, William Karfoot was a major force in the direction of its affairs as the following week the *Chorley Standard* published a letter from Thomas Birtwistle in which he appears to depict Karfoot as the man responsible for the mill's actions, referring to his "handywork.....so similar to his craft."

The dispute was eventually resolved but it illustrated that the Co-operative Mill, at best, was regarded with lukewarm support amongst workers and co-operators in Chorley. A letter to the *Chorley Standard* after the end of the dispute, illustrates this point;

the public know enough already of the so-called Co-operative Mill. I say so-called, because there is not a little of the real principle of co-operation about it. We all know that the principle of co-operation seeks to improve the social condition of the working man. I ask, has the above establishment ever advanced one step in that direction? Let the workpeople,

---

[226] *Chorley Standard* 28 September 1867

some of whom are shareholders, give the answer, and I feel convinced it will be in the negative. [227]

A further letter in the same edition suggested that shareholders should take action;

> I regret, however, the shareholders will not be gulled by them any longer, and next time they have to give an account of their stewardship, to put men in as directors who will not try to impose upon their fellow men.

The second letter writer, signed himself as "A Lover of Truth". He did not want his name known for fear of being "rattened". Webster's Revised Unabridged Dictionary 1913 gives a definition "To deprive feloniously of the tools in one's employment (as by breaking or stealing them) for the purpose of annoying: as to ratten a mechanic who works during a strike". Clearly the climate of fear which was common to much 19th century employment was also present at Chorley's Co-operative Mill. This view of the Co-operative Mill echoes what Hampson described as "the fury with which co-operators attacked the worker-owned joint stock companies" in letters to *The Co-operator*."[228]

This dispute may well have damaged William Karfoot's reputation with some of Chorley's workers and co-operators, but it clearly did no harm in terms of his standing with other shareholders at the Co-operative Mill. In the following year he chaired the half-yearly meeting of shareholders when "the utmost unanimity prevailed at the meeting" although "there was no dividend declared owing to the depreciation of the goods in the market, and to the paying off the loss on last half year."[229] It is somewhat ironic that this is one of the few mentions in newspaper reports to the payment of dividend and no dividend was paid! However, although business was clearly difficult, the mill was not stagnating. Invitations for tenders for flagging, slating,

---

[227] Ibid. 9 November 1867.
[228] Hampson. Op. Cit. 190.
[229] *Chorley Standard* 8 August 1868.

plastering and joinery for an extension to the mill were published and later in the year tenders were sought for plumbing, glazing and painting an extension.[230]

As referred to earlier, in 1869 William Karfoot became the manager of the Co-operative Mill, replacing Ralph Richardson who had held that role for three years, including the acrimonious dispute. At a presentation to mark his departure, Henry Croston, a director and shareholder, emphasised the value of co-operative principles; "England would be a great deal finer country than it is if everybody would try co-operation - he urged all to put down slanderers and backbiters."[231] This is evidence that despite the problems that had been experienced, directors still saw themselves as being in charge of a co-operative business.

Reports about the affairs of the Co-operative Mill were always sporadic and, if anything, became more sporadic in its second decade of business. However, a property valuation for the Improvement Commissioners in 1870 showed that the Co-operative company had six houses on Steeley Lane and a 4.1 acre brickcroft also on Steeley Lane, next to the Co-operative Mill. Traditionally bricks were produced close to where they were to be used. Presumably bricks were made to build or extend the mill and to build their own houses, but possibly also for the houses of retail society members on neighbouring Brook Street.[232] It is clear that a co-operative community was developing in the area between Steeley Lane and Brook Street, given also that a branch store of the retail society operated in Brook Street for a time. Frank Longton thought there might have been something idealistic about the mill's layout as an advertisement had referred to it as "the factory in a garden,"[233] and, as mentioned earlier it was often known as Greenfield Mill. This idealism was similar to that which had sought to turn Birkacre into a Co-operative community. From its Owenite beginnings the Co-operative movement was keen to improve the quality of working-class housing. The reasons were expressed in *The Co-operator*: "It is scarcely possible to estimate

---

[230] Ibid. 25 July and 7 November 1868.
[231] Ibid. 20 March 1869.
[232] Chorley Valuation 1871 LCRO MBCH 36/3.
[233] Longton. Op. Cit. 10.

Co-operation in Chorley 1830-1880

the amount of misery and crime produced by unhealthy houses. The occupants of such houses as we are contemplating, do not live, they only pass the time."[234] Many societies were active in providing housing. In Darwen, for example "by 1910, an estimated 25% of the houses in the borough were either built by, or purchased through the Darwen Co-operative Society."[235] The opportunity to obtain better housing was another incentive for people to become co-operative members and workers, as in the case of the Chorley Co-operative mill.

Reports and statistics on co-operative production businesses came to be provided to annual co-operative congresses. There was no mention of the Chorley Mill. This could be seen as deliberate exclusion of a joint stock venture, however it is known that the retail society did not subscribe to the Co-operative Union, so It may be there was little contact with the national body.

At a half-yearly meeting of shareholders in 1872, it was reported that "the deficit caused by the great fluctuation of prices during the cotton famine was cleared off", it was hoped to start a hundred more looms, interest at 5% had been paid on loans and 5% dividend to shareholders. "A bright prospect was before the shareholders".[236] Allowing for the fact that management reports from both of Chorley's Co-operatives almost always erred on the side of optimism, it would appear that the mill was in a relatively healthy position. The following six months were equally successful; the additional hundred looms were started and forty others were planned. The dividend to shareholders had gone up from 5% to 7.5% and half year profits were £335,[237] originating from cloth sales of £15,447.[238]

1873 saw William Karfoot, on behalf of the Co-operative Mill, in alliance with William Lawrence, the Lyon's Lane millowner, in dispute with the Lancashire and Yorkshire Railway Company over the proposed closure of the level crossing at Chorley Railway Station. The dispute was reported at length in the local press. In

---

[234] *The Co-operator* 9 January 1869
[235] Firth. Op. Cit. 19.
[236] *Chorley Standard* 17 August 1872.
[237] Ibid. 15 February 1873.
[238] Ibid.

John E. Harrison

seeking help from Chorley's Improvement Commissioners Karfoot stated

> The Co-operative Manufacturing Co. Ltd had, as the board were aware, a large tract of land for building upon, and if the road was stopped, this land would be materially affected.[239]

This land was part of the Co-operative Mill site, acquired at the time of the founding of the company, and it was still largely not in use when the company was liquidated. This perhaps endorses Longton's reference to "the factory in a garden."

Karfoot and Lawrence with about 100 others, attacked and destroyed the crossing gates and consequentially were summoned by the railway company for wilful damage. The case against Karfoot was withdrawn and Lawrence was fined a nominal shilling with five shillings damages.[240]

In trading terms, the mid 1870s continued to be a period of optimism for the Co-operative Mill. In February 1875, as well as paying dividend, interest on loans and putting aside money for depreciation,

> The directors also intimate that the subject of extension for spinning will be brought forward, as they are confident that the best opportunity now presents itself. No promotion money nor extra ground rent will be paid; and not less than for £2,000 to £3,000 brought into use that is not at present of any utility. The shareholders will have the preference; afterwards the public, from whom much encouragement has been received.[241]

Quite possibly the intention was to use the adjacent surplus land. The proposal won the support of the shareholders:

---

[239] Ibid. 27 September 1873.
[240] Ibid. 18 October 1873.
[241] Ibid. 20 February 1875

The report was unanimously adopted, and a resolution was passed empowering the directors to proceed with prudence towards enabling the company to spin their own weft so as to use up the capital which is not now of any utility.[242]

The expansion into spinning did not take place, and this would seem to have been due to further industrial disputes and to the downturn in trade. A further dispute with the Weavers' Union blew up in June 1875. Once again it was about payment according to the lists in neighbouring towns. The dispute involved mills across Chorley, but given his role with the local employers' organisation, William Karfoot was on the "front line." He thought "the weavers were asking too much."[243] The view of the President of the Weavers' Union was "From what he had heard of the question from time to time, it lodged more in a place called the Co-operative Mill."[244] "It" in this case being the main source of resistance to the weavers. Karfoot's resistance to the demands of the weavers appeared to reflect badly on co-operation in Chorley. James White of Church was probably a union member.

> He was sorry to hear that the Co-operative Mill was one of the worst they had to bring up, and the President asked if that was the principle of co-operation. He (Mr. White) told them it was not the principle of co-operation, for that was never intended for the pulling down of wages.[245]

The attack was joined by the General Secretary of the Weavers' Union, Mr. Birtwistle, who argued that if Mr. Karfoot had his way the weavers would "suffer a considerable reduction in wages."[246]

A dispute also arose in 1875 involving the Oldham Limiteds which resulted in them being "ranged on the side of the

---

[242] Ibid.
[243] Ibid. 26 June 1875.
[244] Ibid.
[245] Ibid.
[246] Ibid.

capitalists....... even so, many still regarded the Limiteds as an extension of working class control."[247]

The dispute was settled at the end of July. Whether the weavers actually went on strike is not clear, although mills were given notice of strike action. However, what was significant was that the employers accepted the proposal of the Weavers' Association, which must have been seen as a huge defeat for William Karfoot.

The downturn in trade was probably the most telling factor in not only shelving expansion plans, but in the closure of the mill. By May 1876 the *Chorley Standard* was reporting "We understand that the cotton trade in this town is in a very unsatisfactory state, and that several large firms are now working to stock."[248] Optimism must have disappeared; by 1877 an economic depression had begun and manufacturers were cutting wages and reducing hours.[249] In 1878 workers responded with what the *Chorley Standard* called "The Great Strike in the Cotton Trade."[250] By May it was reported that several cotton mills in Bolton had closed as a result of the strike.[251] The following month saw both spinners and weavers in Chorley facing a 10% cut in wage rates.[252] By August it was being reported that "The depression (in the Cotton Trade) is worse every day,[253]" and by October the view was that this depression was the worst that the industry had experienced.[254] The following month there was a more detailed report of the local situation, identifying mills closed, on short time or experiencing strikes.

> In common with the rest of the cotton manufacturing districts of Lancashire, Chorley is unfortunately subject to the general depression in trade; and curtailment of production is the general rule. Most employers in the town have for a long time past

---

[247] Toms. Op. Cit. 8.
[248] *Chorley Standard* 6 May 1876.
[249] Ibid. 1 September 1877.
[250] Ibid. 20 April 1878.
[251] Ibid. 18 May 1878.
[252] Ibid. 29 June 1878.
[253] Ibid. 10 August 1878.
[254] Ibid. 19 October 1878.

experienced the burden of heavy stocks without
any hope of obtaining a market.[255]

There was no mention of the Co-operative Mill, (or of Smethurst's Mills), so it can be assumed that they were still working. However, the employers decided to introduce a four day week.[256] It seems likely that with the mill operating at below full capacity a decision was taken to sublet premises to bring in income, because when the Co-operative Mill was eventually liquidated it was reported that some of its premises were being used by a Tallow Chandler and a Shuttle Manufacturer.

The New Year saw no improvement in the trade depression, and the loss of income was causing considerable suffering among the spinners and weavers and their families. The Poor Law Relieving Officer had between 500 and 600 cases but "it was believed there was double that number in need".[257] As the Depression continued, the Chorley employers decided on a further cut in wage rates[258]. The workers were between the proverbial rock and a hard place, as families would have no resources to support strikers. William Karfoot was once again a leading figure on the Employers' side.[259]

When the weavers met to vote on strike action, the result was so close that it was decided to ballot individual mills. The result was decisively against strike action and individual mill's votes were reported in the *Chorley Standard*. "Greenfield Mill" aka the Co-operative Mill followed the pattern with sixty-nine in favour of staying at work and only five in favour of striking.[260]

The reduction in wages was not sufficient to save some businesses. A week later it was reported that John Gillett's business, the Victoria Saw Mills and Wagon Company and his Cowling Spinning Mill, had failed with liabilities of nearly £7,000.[261] The following month a petition was submitted in the

---

[255] Ibid. 2 November 1878.
[256] Ibid.
[257] Ibid. 18 January 1879.
[258] Ibid. 22 February 1879.
[259] Ibid. 8 March 1879.
[260] Ibid. 15 March 1879.
[261] Ibid. 22 March 1879.

John E. Harrison

Lancashire Court of Chancery for the winding up of the Chorley Co-operative Spinning and Manufacturing Company Limited. Winding up orders were and still are sought by creditors when a company is deemed to be insolvent; that is, unable to pay its debts. The creditors who submitted the winding up petition were:

Jane Watt, 147 Eaves Lane, Chorley. Spinster.
John Karfoot, Lord Street, Chorley. Book Keeper.
Sarah Karfoot, 147, Eaves Lane, Chorley. Spinster.
John Sharples, Red Bank, Chorley. Colliery Manager.
Joseph Gillibrand, 34, Brown Street, Chorley. Overlooker.
William Karfoot, 147, Eaves Lane, Chorley. Mill Manager.
Josiah Taylor, Harpers Lane, Chorley. Foreman Carder.
John Norris, Crosse Hall, Chorley. Tape Sizer.
Matthias Karfoot, Eaves Lane, Chorley. Mill Manager.
William Hopwood, 9, Hope Street, Chorley. Rope Maker.
Peter Molyneaux, 27, Brook Street, Chorley.

The petition was dated the 3rd April 1879 and was subsequently advertised in the *London Gazette*, the *Manchester Guardian* and *Manchester Courier*[262]. It was also reported in the *Preston Guardian*.[263]

---

[262] National Archives BT 31/559/2282
[263] *Preston Chronicle*, 26 Apr. 1879. *British Library Newspapers*, https://link.gale.com/apps/doc/Y3207489926/BNCN?u=lancs&sid=BNCN&xid=cf7d81ca. Accessed 15 Jan. 2020.

> CHORLEY CO-OPERATIVE SPINNING COMPANY.—A petition for the compulsory winding up of the Chorley Co-operative Spinning and Manufacturing Company, Limited, came before Vice-Chancellor Little, sitting in the Palatine Court of Lancaster, Stone-buildings, Lincoln's-inn. The company was constituted as a limited liability company, with a capital of £20,000, divided into shares of £1 each. The object of the company was to buy and sell cotton, and generally to carry on all business incidental to this trade, and about £8000 had been subscribed for this purpose. The petitioners were directors, shareholders, and contributories of the company, who asserted that the company was utterly insolvent, and unable to pay its debts. In support of this view, they stated that actions had been commenced in the Queen's Bench Division to recover sums of money due from the company.— His Honour made an order to wind up the company, conditionally upon an affidavit being produced verifying the facts of the petition.

Winding up the Chorley Co-operative Mill Preston Guardian 26 April 1879

The affidavit which confirmed the position of the company was provided by William Karfoot.

The weavers returned to work briefly to "work up material in stock".[264] This may have been to complete a contract, or simply to ensure that the company's assets were in the best position to be sold by the liquidator. Renewed optimism may have resulted from this because shareholders and creditors met and resolved to form a new company to take over the business, subject to the agreement of the liquidator and mortgagee.[265] This agreement was presumably not obtained as there were no further reports of this proposal. Instead the mill and its contents were auctioned and the advertisement for the auction provided the best description of the Co-operative Mill.

---

[264] *Chorley Guardian* 7 June 1870.
[265] Ibid. 28 June 1879.

John E. Harrison

Sale by Auction: Greenfield Mill -following court order 23rd September. Auction at the Royal Oak Hotel on 6th October 1879 conducted by Messrs William Salesbury and Hamer.- All that brick-built WEAVING SHED, with the Steam Engines, Steam Boiler, Mill Gearing and Machinery, now forming the Green Field Mill, Chorley, belonging to the Chorley Co-operative Spinning and Manufacturing Company Ltd. The buildings 3 storey brick built buildings, forming warehouse, loading place and winding, warping and tape sizing rooms, weaving shed to hold 606 looms, mechanics and joiners shops, storerooms, boiler house, engine house, brick built chimney. Also a brick-built building, now let off to a tallow chandler, also another brick built building let off as a shuttle manufactory.

The driving power etc includes one 30 nominal hp horizontal steam engine, one 30 foot steam boiler, with Henderson's Patent Feed and Hopkinson's Safety Valves, and other fittings, Green's Economiser[266], 60 pipes. The whole of the Mill Gearing, Shafting, steam, gas and water piping; and all other attached fixtures and fittings therein.

The machinery comprises 547 patent power looms. Viz- 60 36 inch reed space, 119 40 inch reed space, 262 47 inch reed space, 45 Of which have twilled motions, and 22 Dobbies attached to them, and 106 50 inch reed space, 2 winding frames, 200 spindles each, one ditto 204 spindles, one ditto 120 spindles, all four and a half inch lift, 8 warping mills with V creels, 2 tape sizing machines, with 60 inch and 40 inch cylinders by Witton and Mills, with size mixing

---

[266] Hopkinsons now part of the Weir Group producing valves at Elland in West Yorkshire- been producing them for 160 years. Greens are World famous for its economisers. It patented the very first economiser in 1845 and is still making them in Wakefield. **Economisers** are mechanical devices intended to reduce energy consumption, or to perform useful function such as preheating a fluid.

apparatus for working the same, 2 cloth plaiting machines, one hydraulic press, one heald(?)- knitting machine, and one 8 spindle sporting?? Machine.

The Mechanics Tools comprise two drilling machines, one single-geared lathe on wood bed, small vertical steam engine, iron saw bench and other attached fixtures.

Also all those EIGHT brick-built DWELLING HOUSES, situate and numbered 41-55 inclusive on Steeley Lane, Chorley. Gross yearly rental £96 4s.

The land forming the site thereof contains 20,893 square yards or thereabouts and is leasehold for a term of 999 years from the first day of November 1861 at a yearly rent of £87 1s 1d.

Two thirds of the land is unbuilt upon and is very suitable for extension purposes or cottage building. The whole of the premises are nearly new, having only worked a few years, are close to the Railway Station, and well-situated for coal. Hands being plentiful.

(My question marks indicate where the text is unclear.)

In such difficult trading times, it was probably not surprising that the auction was unsuccessful. Bidding started at £3,000 and it was withdrawn when bids only reached £5,300.[267] The mill was later sold by tender to a Mr. Brindle of Preston and it re-opened in 1880.[268]

The Co-operative Mill had a limited amount of capital, and this meant that in times of severe depression in the cotton industry it had little to fall back upon. In the volatile conditions of the late 1870s it went the way of many other producer co-operatives and non-co-operative weaving businesses, and failed. However, as indicated it was not only co-operatives that were failing in the severe depression of the late 1870s. In the aftermath of the Co-op Mill's closure, in Chorley alone, Joseph Spedding,

---

[267] *Chorley Guardian* 11 October 1879.
[268] *Chorley Standard* 14 February 1880.

coal agent was declared bankrupt with debts of over £27,000; The Hic Bibi Coal and Canel Company Limited was wound up[269] and Richard Baxendale and Joseph Heald, Wagon Builders failed[270]. At the same time, the *Chorley Guardian* copied a report from the *Manchester Courier* on the state of the cotton trade in the manufacturing districts in which it was reported that the general condition was "unsatisfactory...The spinning departments are running more regularly than the weaving departments." [271]

Birchall argued that the only producer co-operatives which survived this period were largely those that were owned by the wholesale federations and the retail societies, which gave the producer a stable demand for their product.[272] (His argument ignores the continuing success of the Hebden Bridge Fustian Manufacturing Society.) Chorley Co-operative Mill did not have that level of financial and trading support. Although "co-operative" in name and ambition, it never gave a "bonus to labour", and it seems to have survived and failed on its strength as just another small joint stock weaving company. It did not come close to raising its original capital target and therefore never had sufficient capital to develop the site it held and grow to a size and strength which would enable it better to ride the severe economic storms of the late 1870s. Its fortunes were possibly not helped by William Karfoot's high profile disputes with the Weavers Union and his prominence in the local employers' organisation. They did not fit well with perceptions of co-operation as a movement to better the state of working people and it was those disputes which evidenced the loss of the co-operative ideals in the business. However, when Frank Longton wrote his history of local co-operation sixty years after the winding up of the Co-operative Mill, he described it as a co-operative productive cotton mill which attempted to put into practice the profit-sharing principle of co-operation.[273] The venture was co-operative at its inception, although that idealism was largely lost after its first decade of existence.

---

[269] *Chorley Guardian* 3 May 1879.
[270] *Chorley Standard* 19 July 1879.
[271] *Chorley Guardian* 19 July 1879.
[272] Birchall Op. Cit.103.
[273] Longton. Op. Cit. 10.

6

"Our Own", but serving the Community: The Co-operative Hall, Public Baths, Education and Housing

The building of the Co-operative Hall was not just a major achievement for the new retail society; it met a major need in the town as a venue for meetings, concerts and entertainment. Meetings of ratepayers were convened in 1860 to discuss the need for a public hall in Chorley, and how it could be funded. A newspaper report said

> for some time past, the want of a public building, in which public meetings, concerts, lectures, balls etc could be held, has been much felt.[274]

Such meetings could only be held in the County Court, the Sessions Room or in inn rooms and only when rooms were available. A Vestry Meeting was convened to consider the issues and whether to ask the Improvement Commissioners to build a hall, funded from the rates. The Vestry meeting voted not to petition the Improvement Commissioners.[275] The majority of

---

[274] *Preston Guardian* 5 May 1860.
[275] Ibid. 19 May 1860.

ratepayers were reluctant to endorse increased spending and increases in the rates for most issues. The new Town Hall was built almost twenty years later, and was opened in 1879[276].

When the Pilot Industrial Co-operative Society was formed it had to hire rooms for meetings. One such meeting in 1863 was in Pearson's Assembly Rooms.[277] The newspaper report referred to "a new store house now in the course of erection close to the present place of business." The next quarterly meeting referred to the Co-operative Hall "now in the course of erection"[278]. The shop and hall were part of the same project and building. The new premises were opened in January 1864 and were described in detail in the newspaper report.

> The new building includes a public assembly room, which forms the top storey. The second or middle storey is devoted for store-room and offices, and the ground floor is intended for storing and retailing goods. To the building is attached a commodious bakehouse and boilerhouse, and over these is a room in which a kneading apparatus is being fixed, and a steam engine, to be used in kneading and riddling flour, grinding coffee, hoisting etc. The building is at the north-east corner of the market place. The estimated cost, when complete, and including fixtures, is about £1560.[279]

The actual dimensions of the Hall are not known, but an 1880 advertisement described it as "small.[280]

This would be worth about £200,000 at current valuation. The building is still there at the corner of the market place. After the collapse of the Pilot Society, the building was used as a post office and a technical school, before it was taken over by the later

---

[276] *Chorley Standard* 2 August 1879.
[277] *Preston Guardian* 4 July 1863.
[278] Ibid. 10 October 1863.
[279] Ibid. 9 January 1864.
[280] *The Era* 11 April 1880.

Co-operation in Chorley 1830-1880

Chorley Co-operative Society in 1906 and opened to sell drapery, millinery, tailoring and outfitting.[281]

The Chorley Pilot Industrial Co-operative Society built and opened these premises in 1864

Size notwithstanding, the Hall seems to have been well used by other organisations, as well as by the Co-operative Society. Temperance groups used it for lectures, meetings and tea parties and entertainments. Church groups also made use of the Hall. The United Methodist Free Church used it until they had their own church[282]; the Sunday School Union used it for a lecture; a "sacred drama" was presented to liquidate the debt on Heapey Church[283] and a religious service was conducted by the President of the United Free Gospel Churches[284]. There were other occasions when meetings had a more political tone. The meeting to set up a Chorley Branch of the National Reform Union was held there in 1866[285] and a meeting in support of the Disestablishment of the

---

[281] Longton. Op. Cit.35.
[282] *Preston Guardian* 8 April 1865.
[283] *Chorley Standard* 27 April 1867.
[284] Ibid. 7 December 1872.
[285] *Preston Guardian* 10 November 1866

Church of England in 1872.[286] Both meetings had involvement from the Karfoots and William Lawrence. Trade union related meetings also seem to have been held there. In 1866, at a meeting of Operative Weavers, forty to fifty women attended but sat separately from the men[287]. The following year a meeting in support of the Eight Hours Movement was chaired by John Windsor who was associated with the Co-operative Mill[288] and later in the year 200 weavers from that Mill held a strike meeting in the Co-operative Hall.[289] Other activities fall into the miscellaneous category, such as the lecture on phrenology and mesmerism[290], an exhibition of marionette figures[291], a sale of talking parrots and other foreign birds[292], the annual tea of the Loyal Protestant Association of Orangemen[293], a presentation to Army Volunteers[294] and a Grand Gypsy Ball when the retail society was closing[295]. The range and diversity of activities illustrates the important role that the Co-operative Hall played in the Chorley community, prior to the building of the new Town Hall.

The Chorley Pilot Industrial Co-operative Society used spare space in the new building to address another community need in 1864 with the provision of public baths. Baths had become an issue of importance as a consequence of concern about Public Health, both nationally and locally. In the 1840s a spring in Whittle le Woods had been developed into a spa with plunge baths and the waters were apparently taken internally and externally.[296] A further spa was also developed for a short time near Yarrow Bridge, but the first town centre baths seem to have been opened by a Mr. Livesey in Chapel Street. Hot and cold

---

[286] *Chorley Standard* 30 November and 7 December 1872.
[287] Ibid. 12 May 1866.
[288] Ibid. 16 February 1867.
[289] Ibid. 28 September 1867.
[290] Ibid. 29 September 1866.
[291] Ibid. 24 November 1866.
[292] Ibid. 9 November 1872.
[293] Ibid. 16 November 1872.
[294] *Preston Guardian* 26 January 1878.
[295] *Chorley Guardian* 25 October 1879.
[296] Harrison, John, 2010. Campaign for Public Baths in Victorian Chorley in Lancashire History Quarterly Vol 13 No1.

baths were provided using water from Chorley Waterworks. The bathing facilities in the Co-operative Hall building seem to have been provided to replace Livesey's baths. "Pro Bono Publico", in a newspaper letter, described Livesey's baths as "inadequate" and "shortly to be private," and claimed that public baths were desired by doctors, surgeons, clergymen and hundreds of the town's inhabitants to benefit the health of the community.[297] The letter was responded to in an editorial in the same edition of the *Chorley Standard*: "It is of the first importance that due facilities for cleanliness and the preservation of health be affected."[298] The issue was then picked up by the town's medical officer, John Rigby in his quarterly report: "The baths would be of some service in the treatment of some forms of disease".[299] A petition in favour of public baths presented at the same meeting of the Improvement Commissioners was described as "the most numerous and respectably signed petition yet put before the Commission."[300] However the Improvement Commission was notoriously reluctant to commit to any expense at the cost of the ratepayers and after what was described as "desultory conversations", deferred any decision for 6 months. It should be noted that although there had been a typhus epidemic in Preston in 1862, there did not appear to be a particular health crisis driving this campaign at that time. Rigby had reported positively on the health of the town in his report. However, this was in the middle of the Cotton Famine with all its hardships and fears, and I have suggested elsewhere that alongside the re-establishment of Dispensary premises the previous year, the opening of public baths could be seen as an "alternative, or complimentary means of caring for the health of the poor",[301] when they could not afford coal or clothes and did not have the means to heat water to effectively wash clothes. In this context, public baths were the

---

[297] *Chorley Standard* 24 September 1864.
[298] Ibid.
[299] Ibid. 1 October 1864.
[300] Ibid.
[301] Harrison, J. E., 1983. The Development of Medical Care and Public Health in Nineteenth Century Chorley. Unpublished Msc. thesis. University of Manchester. 226.

"means whereby standards of cleanliness could be improved, thus reducing the opportunities for what was seen as the generation of disease by filth."[302]

The campaign continued with a public meeting and further newspaper letters but elicited no support from the Improvement Commission. Instead, it was the Chorley Pilot Industrial Co-operative Society that responded, albeit not on a large scale. The *Preston Guardian* reported that at their next quarterly meeting, William Karfoot, as Chairman:

> stated that the establishment of public baths in connection with the society was likely to prove a success, and several parties had signified their intention to become annual subscribers. The prices had not yet been fixed, but accommodation would be afforded for hot, cold, tepid and shower baths....... he had no doubt that they would be properly appreciated, and that substantial benefits would be derived therefrom, as they would no doubt be patronised by others as well as by the members of the store.[303]

By the following March it was reported that bathing was now possible at the Co-operative Stores where one bathroom, containing a shower and a shallow bath was available on Sundays and in the early morning.[304] However, "Ratepayer", the letter writer who reported this, also described queues and delays, and concluded that "baths and bathers have no chance of success under such circumstances." Clearly any impact on the overall health of the town would have been minimal. However the provision of public baths by the Chorley Pilot Industrial Co-operative Society is testimony not just to the optimism which saw it develop down various avenues, including new branches, a library and reading room and the provision of housing, but also testimony to a

---

[302] Ibid. 227.
[303] *Preston Guardian*. 31 December 1864.
[304] *Chorley Standard* 25 March 1865.

willingness to meet and serve community needs which were not being addressed by the Improvement Commissioners.

One of the most important features of the Rochdale model of Co-operation was educational provision. Gurney reminds us that

> Libraries and reading rooms had long occupied a prominent place in the traditions of radical education; in 1842, for example, twenty Owenite branches had libraries throughout the country.[305]

This commitment was picked up by the Co-operative Movement. Turnbull and Southern suggest that "the commitment to education was particularly evident in the early societies in Lancashire."[306] This usually consisted of libraries, newsrooms and publications, but it could also include lectures and adult education classes. By 1879, there were at least fifty-five libraries and newsrooms across Lancashire, Yorkshire and Durham, and thirty-six of those were in Lancashire.[307] This figure may underestimate by not recognising provision that had been established but had subsequently closed for whatever reason. Everitt's list does not include Chorley[308]. This may have been because there seems to have been little connection with the Co-operative Union.

The aim was to create better citizens who were literate and could usefully contribute to the running of Societies, but there was also the subtext of engaging working people in activities away from the beer shop and public house. The Co-operative Union suggested that 2.5% of a Society's profits be allocated to educational purposes, but a survey in 1884 showed that only 37% of societies allocated money for Education and of those, not all by any means, allocated 2.5% of profits. The Chorley Pilot Society only started to look at Educational issues five years after its foundation. The idea of a newsroom was raised but deferred to the next quarterly meeting whilst the possible use of a corn

---

[305] Gurney. Op. Cit. 32-3.
[306] Turnbull and Southern. Op. Cit. 29.
[307] Gurney. Op. Cit. 32-3.
[308] Everitt. Op. Cit. 264.

John E. Harrison

mill was discussed.[309] This may not have been due to a lack of enthusiasm but because there were different views about how to proceed. At the next meeting there was "considerable discussion" and Samuel Fairbrother proposed an allocation of 2.5% of profits. This was defeated by an amendment moved by William Karfoot that proposed

> the use of two ante-rooms over the tailoring department, with gas and all necessary fittings, be set apart, free of cost, to those members who are desirous that a newsroom and a library should be opened.[310]

Members were to provide their own papers but religious papers were to be excluded.

There appeared to be no Education Budget, but by the next quarterly meeting 400 volumes had been purchased. The library was not yet operational however because "chapel people" had been using the ante-room on Sunday and Monday evenings and occasionally on other nights and it was not seen as appropriate to pass through the room to the library. The "chapel people" were about to move out, so they could then "see how it is patronised."[311]

A Tea Meeting was held later in the year and the guest speaker, Mr. Slater of Bury, spoke of the importance of the newsroom and library.

> The working man could go after a hard day's work and sit and read the daily and weekly papers, instead of spending all of his time in the public house.[312]

This seems to have helped to give momentum to the project. (Mr. T. Slater of Bury presented a paper on "Co-operation and Education" as part of an important discussion on education at

---

[309] *Chorley Standard* 6 January 1866.
[310] Ibid. 7 April 1866.
[311] Ibid. 7 July 1866
[312] Ibid. 8 December 1866.

Co-operation in Chorley 1830-1880

the Co-operative Congress in Manchester in June 1870[313]). At the Annual Meeting the following month, a committee was formed "to organise the working of a library."[314]

One of the Committee members was William Carr and he was a very enthusiastic supporter of educational issues. At the following quarterly meeting he said

> he felt ashamed of the position of the Co-operative Society with regard to the Educational Department. If they looked around among other co-operatives they would find that in this respect Chorley was the very lowest and hindermost.

He advocated the establishment of a reading room that had more than the current provision of the fortnightly *Co-operator* and the weekly *Chorley Standard,* and that it be funded with £30 from the Management Fund. He was supported by Mr Wilkinson who thought that

> it was necessary to have a reading room where the members, instead of being isolated and distant, could be able to converse upon all the social and moral objects connected with the human family.

He also favoured providing a night school. William Karfoot supported the proposal in principle, but was cautious about funding.

> They must bear in mind that another panic might come and persons would want to withdraw their capital, but they would not be able to find the money all at once.

His suggestion, of £7 10s to be allocated for half a year to fund a reading room, was carried and a committee was formed to take the

---

[313] Everitt Op. Cit. 69.
[314] *Chorley Standard* 5 January 1867.

reading room forward.[315] Later in the year, presumably having seen how the library and reading room were operating, when a special meeting was convened to approve new rules for the Society, it was decided to adopt the principle of allocating 2.5% of net profits to educational purposes.[316] This clearly reflects strength of support, but it is also indicative of the financial success of the Society at that time, when its sales and membership were growing and it was expanding in terms of departments and branches.

Educational provision was seen as an attractive feature in the "offer" to encourage new members. The following year, a newspaper announcement said the library would open at 6pm, had a "good selection of first-class new works" as well as others that had been donated and was free to both members and their families.[317]

Co-operative Societies spent "a considerable part of their educational funds "[318] subsidising tea parties and lectures, usually held in the winter months and serving non-alcoholic drinks. This was a propaganda exercise that had been previously used by Chartists and Owenites and was particularly popular in Lancashire and Yorkshire. Music and dancing were offered to attract people.

In 1871 the Chorley Pilot Society offered a series of "popular lectures over the winter months." They were launched at a tea party and concert on the previous Christmas Eve, chaired by G H Lightoller, a leading millowner. He emphasised that the talks were to be non-controversial and a means of material improvement. The launch was poorly attended, perhaps because it was Christmas Eve![319] However, the programme of nine lectures was "greatly appreciated and well attended".[320] The lectures were to be non-sectarian, although at least two were given by ministers. The subjects of the ones known fitted into Lightoller's prescription; "Real worth in Humble Life, of men who have risen"; "The materials of which men are made with a few specimens from the factory"; "Rocks and Pilots on the Voyage of Life." Further

---

[315] Ibid. 6 April 1867.
[316] Ibid. 30 November 1867.
[317] Ibid. 21 March 1868.
[318] Gurney. Op Cit. 67
[319] *Chorley Standard* 31 December 1870.
[320] Ibid. 11 March 1871

support from the factory owners of Chorley was evident in John Thom of Birkacre chairing one of the lectures.

The lecture series was a success for the Society and its Education Committee, although the latter seems to have trouble convening meetings. It was suggested that this may have been down to members being disgruntled at being overruled by the main committee, but it was suggested that paying members to attend would be an encouragement. It was agreed that 3s 6d would be shared amongst those attending each Education committee meeting.[321]

Members might well have hoped to build on this success. However, educational affairs declined with the declining fortunes of the Society. At its peak, the allocation of 2.5% of net profits per quarter produced £9 13s 6d.[322] By 1873 it had more than halved to £4 14s.[323] Probably as a consequence of this declining budget, the Committee was of the opinion that the reading room "was not considered to be in a satisfactory state" and proposed that reading room members be asked to pay a shilling per year.[324] At the next quarterly meeting it was revealed that apart from Committee members, only one other member had offered to pay the subscription. The room cost £20 per year and so it was decided to close the reading room. At the same meeting it was decided to limit the opening of the baths.[325] This was a shrinking society, and the loss of the reading room was part of that larger picture. A contributing factor to its closure may well have been the suggestion that it was associated with trouble making teetotallers. In 1871 it had been alleged that Society officers went around asking teetotallers to sit on committees and that "the mischief was concocted in the newsroom by the few teetotallers who met there".[326]

The last 2.5% of net profit allocated to the Educational Department appears to have been made at that meeting. The library may well have continued but with no money for new

---

[321] Ibid. 7 January 1871.
[322] Ibid. 9 January 1869.
[323] Ibid. 5 April 1873.
[324] Ibid. 5 July 1873.
[325] Ibid. 11 November 1873.
[326] Ibid. 7 October 1871

books. It should be noted that this was neither the first nor the only Educational provision for working men in the town. Most would not have been able to afford the twelve shillings per year subscription to the Union Library in Back Mount, but many will have patronised the Mechanics Institute founded in 1844. This had a library, with 900 books, and provided night school classes and lectures.

Another important part of the "offer" to encourage Co-operative Society membership was housing. The Rochdale Pioneers had seen this as a stage in creating a community in which members might live; a continuation of the Owenite vision. Indeed, this was their second aim, after establishing a store. However, house building required more capital and the first Co-operative houses were only started to be built in Rochdale by a joint stock co-operative company in 1861. Later, in 1867 the Pioneers built a co-operative estate of eighty-four houses.[327]

In the previous chapter I have referred to housing provided by the Co-operative Mill in Chorley. The Pilot Industrial Co-operative Society began to address this issue at a tea party in 1867.[328] By law it was only able to make loans at that time.[329] However, later in the year an amendment to the Industrial and Provident Societies Act empowered societies to build and sell cottages for members.[330] Land was obtained at the beginning of the following year to build a branch store and erect houses.[331] This may well have been in Brooke Street. From April to August an announcement was repeated in the *Chorley Standard* inviting Society members to inspect the plans for cottages and terms of payment. The following year tenders were invited to erect cottages in Brooke Street[332] and reference was made to two cottages recently built in High Street.[333] How many cottages were built and where they were precisely is not known.

---

[327] Birchall. Op. Cit. 50.
[328] *Chorley Standard* 27 April 1867.
[329] Ibid. 6 July 1867.
[330] Ibid. 5 October 1867.
[331] Ibid. 4 January 1868.
[332] Ibid. 15 May 1869
[333] Ibid. 9 October 1869.

7

The Decline of the Chorley Pilot Industrial Co-operative Society

Frank Longton in his history of the Chorley Co-operative Society wrote that the earlier retail co-operative, the Chorley Pilot Industrial Co-operative Society, closed in 1873. This was incorrect as it traded up to 1880. Given that major inaccuracy, in looking at the growth and decline of the Society, it is necessary to check other information and to consider his argument that its failure was perhaps because the people running it "lacked business ability, knowledge or training."[334]

Local newspapers and occasionally co-operative newspapers provide the only sources of information about the Chorley Pilot Industrial Co-operative Society. It would appear that none of the Society's own records have survived. However, such was the local newspaper coverage, that with only a few gaps, a quarter by quarter and year by year picture is provided. The foundation of this was the quarterly financial report. This appeared to be a copy of what was produced for the members of the society and was usually read out at the meeting, often by the Secretary or an auditor. Sales and profit figures were provided for the last quarter, and whilst the Society was growing these figures would be compared favourably with those of the previous quarter, or of

---

[334] Longton. Op. Cit. 10.

John E. Harrison

the same quarter in the previous year. Figures for contributions and withdrawals would also be given and usually a figure for the current capital of the business. (The latter ceased to be provided in the 1870s as the business went into decline.) It was not usual for total membership numbers to be given, but again during the period of growth, numbers of new members and members leaving the Society were often given.

Year	Membership	Annual Sales	Annual Profits	Capital
1861	36	£3181		
1862	430	£9528	£118	£2068
1863	500	£8973		£2528
1864	500	£10520	£539	£3820
1865	630	£15485	£873	£4672
1866	900	£21448	£1231	£6462
1867	1030	£24154	£1595	£9084
1868	977	£29678	£1879	£10070
1869		£27534	£1776	
1870	960	£25000		£9534
1871	1000	£25267	£1850	£10547
1872	716	£25819	£1894	£10722
1873	1007*			
1874	650			
1875	629			
1876				
1877	463			
1878	459			
1879				
1880				

*Figure in Co-operators Handbook and may relate to a previous year.

From the members' perspective the most important piece of information was the figure for the dividend to be given to members on their purchases over the past quarter. It would be arrived at by deducting from the profit, amounts for interest on capital, the reserve fund, the depreciation account and sometimes for the education fund and suspense account. In the early days of the Society when reports were only to be found in the *Preston Guardian*, and occasionally during its decline in the late 1870s, the financial details were all that was reported. (Presumably no reporter had attended the quarterly meeting, and the Society sent its financial report to the newspaper). In most other circumstances a more detailed report was provided which would often include a speech by the chairman of the meeting. On occasions where there was a dispute, the Chorley newspapers frequently provided what seemed to be a verbatim report of what each named protagonist said. Disputes sometimes generated letters to the newspapers and these were to be found in both the Preston and Chorley newspapers.

The announcements columns of the Chorley newspapers from time to time contained information about events such as meetings, tea parties, sales of stock, opening arrangements for the co-operative baths and departmental changes.

Data about the annual performance of the Society was best provided during the 1860s whilst the business was growing. This was usually reported as part of the July quarterly meeting and included total membership, annual sales, annual profits and capital. Occasionally this information has been gleaned from reports given, either by the Secretary or Chairman, on a special occasion such as a Tea Party or the opening of the Co-operative Hall.

I have already characterised the 1860s as a period of growth and the 1870s as one of decline. This chapter will attempt to illustrate that and pinpoint the turning point and the factors which led to the decline of the Society. When the Society in 1876 was undergoing several difficulties, one of the members, Mr. Meakin, attempted to rally the members by reminding them that "There was a panic about eight years ago, and the Society weathered the storm"[335] This would indicate that perhaps 1868

---

[335] *Chorley Standard* 27 May 1876.

was a turning point. (The significance of "weathered the storm" would not be lost on those members who remembered that it was the Pilot that weathered the Storm Lodge of the Oddfellows that had been instrumental in founding the Society.)

Statistics would seem to confirm that 1868 was the turning point. Membership peaked in 1867 at 1030, dropping to 977 in 1868. This was the first annual fall in membership, although there had been a static period at around 500 members during the Cotton Famine years, 1863 and 1864. Annual sales certainly peaked in 1868 at £29,678 and whilst annual profits in the same year of £1879 were marginally exceeded in 1872 (£1894), a plateau had been reached. Similarly, the business's capital after a period of rapid growth, reached £10,070 in 1868 and only grew to £10,722 in 1872. That notwithstanding, this was a remarkable achievement for a business which at the end of its first quarter in 1861 had eighty four members, capital of £163 and weekly sales of £20.[336] The subsequent growth was marked by many developments including branches in Adlington, Whittle le Woods, Crosse Hall, Brook Street and Park Road, a bakehouse, a clothing club, a Co-operative Hall, a Clogging Branch, Public Baths, Tea Parties, a new store in Adlington, a library and newsroom, funeral service, and cottages built and sold for members. The Society had its own motto, "Our Own" which was displayed on a banner at events.

Very little is known about the branches, other than the sales figures reported in quarterly returns. In general, they seem to have been created as part of the optimistic expansionist phase of the mid-1860s. Firth noted that in North East Lancashire, branch formation was something which took place early in a society's life, "often almost as soon as the main store was set up"[337].

At least one other branch was considered in Euxton. In Adlington, the original shop seems to have been at the edge of the township, bordering Heath Charnock, at 3 Brook Street[338], and was presumably associated with Brook Mill. The owners of the mill in the 1860s and early 1870s were Cook and Slater, Cotton Manufacturers. In 1872 the *Co-operative News* published

---

[336] *Preston Guardian* 9 January 1864
[337] Firth. Op. Cit.7.
[338] Slater's Directory 1871.

a fulsome obituary for James Slater of Adlington, an earnest co-operator, who was an overlooker in a cotton mill.[339] The mill changed ownership in 1872 so James may have been a partner in the business up until his death. As early as 1866, Adlington members were seeking a new shop because of the distance to be travelled from Lower Adlington. In response, a new shop was opened near the Elephant and Castle public house in 1867. Given that the Chorley Society's records make no mention of two branches in Adlington at this time, it is presumed that the Brook Street shop closed.

The town branches in Chorley in Crosse Hall, Brook Street and Park Road were located close to textile industrial sites with adjacent housing. The Whittle, Crosse Hall and Brook Street branches had relatively short lives. Only the closure of the Whittle branch was reported. These were a Victorian version of "pop up shops", probably operating in cottages, like the beginnings of most retail co-operatives. As the Chorley Society entered more difficult trading times from 1868 onwards, there was consolidation around Chorley and Adlington but as will be seen in the histories of local village co-operatives in the Appendix, contact with these co-operatives was maintained by Thomas Hodgkinson and William Karfoot as part of the wider Co-operative community.

The core business was groceries, particularly at the main branch in Chorley and at Adlington, but other departments included a bakery, clogging, tailoring and drapery. Mention of these other departments and other branches tended to only occur when problems occurred with fluctuations in trade.

The problems of the Pilot Industrial Co-operative Society in 1868 were multi-faceted but seem to have started with the underperforming Drapery Department. In the previous year auctioneers were engaged to sell off drapery stock consisting of "Dress Goods, Shawls, Mantles, Millinery, Flannels, and a great variety of other useful goods." This was to be sold "without reserve."[340] It would seem that this was stock which the Society could not sell by normal means. Later in the year, the secretary

---

[339] *Co-operative News* 27 April 1872.
[340] *Chorley Standard* 18 May 1867.

reported that a loss of £37 had been incurred on the sale of the drapery stock.[341] This was not just a significant loss in itself, but the underperformance of the Drapery Department was offered as one of the reasons why the dividend was not as high as members might have wished. (The issue of low dividends was an ongoing and corrosive issue through most of the life of this society.)

Having sold off old stock by auction, the Society re-stocked both the Drapery and Tailoring Departments as can be seen from the following advertisement which first ran in February 1868, and was repeated for the next three months:

> The attention of members of the public is directed to the advantages offered in the Tailoring and Drapery departments. These departments have recently been supplied with a good selection of the newest and most fashionable goods, which have been purchased since the *late decline. The remainder of the stock has been re-marked at a corresponding reduction in price.* The Tailoring department has been put under *new and efficient management,* and with *ample capital* at our disposal, and taking advantage of all the recent improvements, we are in a position to supply goods as cheap, if not cheaper, than any respectable house in the trade.[342]

My italics highlight the phrases that tell us that these were two departments that had been struggling; the society had cut its losses but had reinvested in new stock. It was almost certainly the issue with the Drapery Department that raised concerns with the members and led to "a crowded attendance of members, who manifested great interest in the welfare of the society" at the next quarterly meeting.[343](Normally attendances were described as "small"). Issues were raised with the committee about stock taking and the valuation of stock; criticisms were made by the

---

[341] Ibid. 6 July 1867.
[342] Ibid. 22 February 1868.
[343] Ibid. 4 April 1868.

committee of the former management. The Secretary, Thomas Hodgkinson came in for criticism and was not fully supported by the Chairman, William Karfoot. Hodgkinson seemed to feel that he was coming in for unjust criticism:

> There had been a deficiency for some time in this department, and it seemed strange to him the question had never been asked before. It seemed to him to be a concocted affair. It seemed to him to be a sore place all at once.[344]

He reported that the "deficiency" in the Drapery Department had been £170.

Blame was thrown around in the meeting. The Committee knew of the problem and were blamed; William Karfoot was blamed as a committee member; the members were blamed for pressurising the committee to pay a higher dividend. There was clearly an issue about the buying in of the right stock, in the right quantity and at the right price. In future, the manager, Mr. Critchley, was to be the Society's buyer.

The issue still rankled with the membership of the Chorley Pilot Industrial Co-operative Society and this prompted a series of letters to the Editor of the *Chorley Standard*. Accusations were made that the Drapery Department had been running a deficit since 1864, and that the committee had connived at hiding the loss in the accounts. "The loss arose through dealing with travellers and giving too high a price for the goods."[345] The solution would be to deal more with the Wholesale Society.

In defence of the Secretary, the argument broadened: "The sore lies here, the secretary is an abstainer, and the treasurer a publican."[346] The treasurer, Henry Whittaker of the Prince of Wales Hotel, responded with his own letter to the Editor, as did the auditors who both defended their reporting and confirmed that because the Society had reserves sufficient to meet the deficit "no apprehensions need be entertained as to the stability

---

[344] Ibid.
[345] Ibid. 18 April 1868. Letter from "A Late Member of the Committee".
[346] Ibid.

of the society".[347] This would seem to be the first occasion that it was necessary to reassure the members about the future of the business.

Others feared that worse news was to be uncovered:

> I am afraid there are 'breakers ahead.' One dismal fact has already been revealed, and the experience of the past few years tells us that when facts of this kind pop up in connection with public companies, it is only the precursor of something worse. I hope it may not prove so in this case. 'Tis true last week you published a statement of the auditors as to its position; but did that statement prove anything good? Not at all. The figures may be balanced up nicely for their inspection, but who values the stocks - the committee or their officers?[348]

This writer also returned to the issue of having a publican as Treasurer:

> and I would ask, are the leading members of the committee the best men whom the members could get? How have they managed other concerns that they have had to do with? How is it that the members are satisfied with having a publican for its treasurer? Is it in keeping with the objects of the society that such should be the case? I think every well-meaning member of the Society will answer no, and I say no too. The publican, I believe, as a rule, gets his living by that which the poor man and his family should subsist upon and be clothed with - therefore it is not fitting that one of this trade should be one of the principal officers of a

---

[347] Ibid. 25 April 1868. Letter from George Fairbrother and Mathias Karfoot (Present Auditors) and James Sandham (Late Auditor)
[348] Ibid. 2 May 1868. Letter from "Enquirer".

society whose mission is to elevate and bless the working man.[349]

Many supporters of Co-operation took the view that consumption of alcohol was out of control.

> The whole life of the working class is surrounded by drink - drink at footings, drink at sick clubs, drink at morning, noon and night. They drink one third of their earnings.[350]

It then followed that poverty was in a large part seen as being due to a morally reprehensible lifestyle in which intoxicating drink was the major cause. This view was widely expressed and echoed in the following "It is to the expenditure of the working class on intoxicating drinks that we chiefly owe our pauperism and crime."[351]

A further letter from "A Large Shareholder" took issue with the letter from "a late member of the Committee", as he accused the committee of creating a "pernicious mist" and "dark portentous clouds". "A Large Shareholder" argued that the original problem in the Drapery Department had been investigated and resolved with no blame to any individual. The fault, he argued, lay with members not taking sufficient interest in the issue and not patronising the Department. He felt that the changes made by the Committee had dealt with the issue and described someone who "despitefully vilifies his own stores" as "a bad bird who fouls his own nest." As a result of "A Late Member of the Committee" crying "wolf", it appeared that some members had withdrawn their savings from the society at a cost to them of 5%. It was conceded that there had been a need to remove those committee men who were "clinging to office". In this there is agreement with "Enquirer" another letter-writer, however "A Large Shareholder" believed that the new committee members were "men of ability, honesty and business habits." He felt that the society was on

---

[349] Ibid.
[350] *The Co-operator* 1 January 1870.
[351] Ibid. 20 February 1869.

sound foundations and would go on to flourish, and therefore, far from withdrawing money and support, there was a strong argument for people to join and invest.[352]

"Father of a small family" continued the attack on the publican treasurer,

> the objects of co-operation, and the objects of the bitter beer seller, are so diametrically opposed to each other, that we cannot support the one without neglecting the other; consequently, I think the store is the place that the working man ought to support.[353]

He also pointed out that it took five quarters to turn over the stock of the drapery department when they had stock to the value of £1,600 and were only selling £300 worth per quarter.

Others had realised that whatever the rights and wrongs of the situation, the debate had opened serious wounds.

> The letter of a 'Late Committee Man' was a great mistake, the expressions of anger, and ill-feeling displayed, were incompatible with a charitable disposition or courteous behaviour, and the insinuations so freely used are very objectionable....... it is very desirable that we should be careful not to bring different creeds, opinions etc into collision; what have we as a society of co-operators to do with abstainers, or temperance men, publicans or private individuals, politics or religion should never be introduced, let us have the right man in the right place, and look entirely, singly, and solely to the benefit and prosperity of the society.[354]

That notwithstanding, it was decided in 1870 that instead of having a publican as treasurer, the society would engage the

---

[352] *Chorley Standard* 2 May 1868. Letter from "A Large Shareholder."
[353] Ibid. 2 May 1868. Letter from "Father of a small family."
[354] Ibid. 2 May 1868. Letter from "A Member of the Society."

services of a bank, the choice being between the Lancaster Bank and the Manchester and Salford Bank.[355]

The fortunes of the Drapery department improved later in the year, but serious damage had been done to confidence in the Society and its leaders, and relationships amongst those running the Society had been damaged to an irreparable degree. The latter was illustrated later in the same year when Mr. Fairbrother (probably Samuel, a leading Chorley co-operator) accused the committee and William Karfoot of being financially imprudent and of stretching the rules to make the dividend higher than it should have been.[356] However, whatever the personal disputes, it was the loss of members' confidence that was most telling. The Co-operative ship had been torpedoed below the water line. Chris Wrigley wrote:

> One of the central business issues facing co-operative societies from their beginnings: confidence. In the societies rested many hopes and aspirations of their members, but high among these was a safe means of financial betterment. Quite apart from the divi (dividend), for many people a sound co-operative society represented a safe location for savings.[357]

After the Drapery Department crisis, confidence in the Chorley Pilot Industrial Co-operative Society was on the wane, and never recovered.

The debate over the failings of the Drapery department had exposed most of the issues which contributed to the decline and liquidation of the Chorley Pilot Industrial Co-operative Society in the second decade of its existence. Whilst turnover and profit figures grew, the performance of different departments and branches fluctuated and this led to departmental re-organisations

---

[355] *Preston Guardian* 8 January 1870.
[356] *Chorley Standard* 4 July 1868.
[357] Wrigley, Chris, 2009. "The Commemorative Urge: the co-operative movement's collective memory" in <u>Consumerism and the Co-operative Movement in Modern British History</u> edited by Black, Lawrence and Robertson, Nicole.158. Manchester.

and closures of branches from time to time. During the period of growth, the failings of some parts of the business were less apparent to the members, or were passed over, not being regarded as serious issues.

Financial performance data of individual departments was not provided in the quarterly reports and only loss figures were occasionally provided when a department was in crisis.

It was surely a major factor in the success of the retail co-operative in the 1860s that for most of the decade it had stable operational management through the Secretary, Thomas Hodgkinson and the manager, John Critchley. That stability was lost when they gave up their roles and the following period was characterised by various management changes. One can only speculate as to whether these were the cause or result of the decline of the retail society.

John Critchley resigned in the aftermath of an alleged embezzlement case against an employee. The case was withdrawn by the Society before it could be heard by John Rigby JP, Co-operative member and landlord. Mr. Rigby was highly critical of the conduct of the Society;

> A very extraordinary mode of proceeding......the case as brought before me the other day appeared as clear a case of embezzlement as there possibly could be. I don't think the course taken by the committee will be satisfactory to the shareholders.......I am quite satisfied that the prisoner has acted unfairly towards his employers.... Whatever can have induced the committee to give up the prosecution?[358]

Thomas Hodgkinson argued that the Committee thought that there was no clear case. Dr. Rigby was unconvinced;

> Really I cannot see what is to become of your company if you compromise cases of this kind. The Committee are accountable to the Shareholders

---

[358] *Chorley Standard* 19 August 1871

and I expect they will make a proper investigation into this matter. It is not your own property, but it is property that belongs to very industrious poor men'.[359]

John Critchley subsequently offered his resignation which was accepted. He was replaced by one of the leading members, Samuel Fairbrother, an overlooker at Lawrence's mill, but he lasted less than a year, to be replaced by an "experienced manager."

Thomas Hodgkinson resigned in 1872. He had come under some criticism over the failings of the Drapery Department in 1868, including comments from William Karfoot, and had had to defend himself and the committee from the sharp criticisms of John Rigby JP over the collapsed embezzlement prosecution in 1871.

He was a member of the Temperance Union and helped to found a Coffee Tavern in Chorley in 1878.[360] (He was honorary secretary and director). In the same year he was a member of an unsuccessful slate (list) of Liberal Coffee Tavern Candidates who sought election to the Improvement Commission that governed the town's affairs. He continued to be a member of the Co-operative Society and contributed to debates about its affairs as it declined through the 1870s.

The most common issue debated by the members throughout the history of the Society was that of the low level of dividend when compared to other societies. Many historians of the Co-operative Movement from Beatrice Webb onwards have expressed the view that workers were largely attracted to the movement by what they could get out of it, and most of the evidence from discussions at meetings of the Chorley Pilot Society would seem to support that view. That might seem to be a materialistic argument, but the reality of working class life was that families "negotiated a narrow path between scarcity and survival and found the 'divi' invaluable".[361] Its use varied from family to family, depending

---

[359] Ibid.
[360] Ibid. 2 March 1878.
[361] Gurney. Op. Cit. 64.

on household circumstances, more particularly employment and wage levels, as well as health and family size.

In paying low dividends, it appears that the Chorley Society was acting on the advice of Henry Pitman, editor of *The Co-operator*, the movement's newspaper. He advised Chorley members:

> I must warn you against over-valuing your stock to make large dividends the first few quarters, as it will have a very bad effect if, after having paid 1s 7d in the £ if you have to pay 3d, which has been the case with a society in our neighbourhood.[362]

Peter Firth found three key factors influencing dividend policy in the East Lancashire Co-operatives.

- Local trading conditions: ie. if the Society was well patronised, dividend would be high.
- Local employment conditions: in poor trade, dividend was sometimes reduced to depress prices and accommodate loss of earnings.
- The extent to which the Society wished to indicate "dynamism", a high dividend indicating a thriving and well-run store.[363]

The level of dividend was never high, and was usually low when compared to other societies. This was probably due to a combination of factors over the years. Throughout the period there was strong local competition and during the Cotton Famine and the increasingly difficult trading conditions of the mid to late 1870s, earnings of members were reduced through wage rate reductions and unemployment. However, there were some accusations that the committee had "protected" the dividend. For example, in 1868, the committee was accused of allowing more profit on the drapery department than there actually was to raise the dividend.[364]

---

[362] *The Co-operator* August 1862.
[363] Firth Op. Cit. 25
[364] *Chorley Standard* 4 July 1868.

A typical debate that occurred in 1865 was initiated by John Taylor[365], one of the members, who said

> He was in the habit of reading newspaper reports of the transactions of other societies, and he found that though they had all expenses similar to their own, yet the dividends were considerably larger. He was at a loss to account for this.

Samuel Fairbrother was chairing the meeting and responded

> that the reason why their dividend did not get up to those of other places was because they did not patronise to the same extent those articles that did pay dividends. Those persons that went there and purchased grain, and went elsewhere to buy coffees, tea, etc, actually sacrificed dividends, taking the dividend from those people that bought teas and so forth to pay up the losses which were incurred by them purchasing nothing but bread stuffs.

The problem was perhaps best summed up nearly a hundred years later in 1955 by an independent commission set up to report on the state of the co-operative movement and its trade:

> In a co-operative society the members are both consumers, who want lower prices, and members, who want a higher dividend; and we do not clearly know how they weigh their claims in these respective roles.[366]

Clearly the Chorley Pilot Industrial Co-operative Society could not offer both lower prices and higher dividends!

---

[365] Ibid. 8 April 1865
[366] Quoted in Walton, John K., 2009. "The Post War decline of the British Retail Co-operative Movement: nature, causes and consequences" in <u>Consumerism and the Co-operative Movement in Modern British History.</u> Edited by Black, Lawrence and Robertson, Nicole. 25 Manchester.

John E. Harrison

Firth believed that "membership was seen as a commitment to the co-operative ethic and a tacit understanding not to revert to private traders."[367] If that was true in North East Lancashire, it was certainly not true of many of the members of the Chorley Pilot Industrial Co-operative Society. There was recurring criticism of members by the committee and officers, in that some did not shop at the Co-op at all, whilst others did not make the Co-operative shop their only place to shop. There certainly appears to have been a significant body of members who were happy to invest in the Society and receive regular payments of 5% interest but did not patronise its shops and departments. William Karfoot, when chairing a meeting in 1877 said that "scarcely half of the members of the Society traded at the stores".[368] This was confirmed in a report in *Co-operative News* which said that

> Number of members 497, of whom only 243, or 48% have brought in checks......52% of the members are non-purchasing.[369]

The reasons for this lack of support were probably threefold. Chorley was and is a market town and had many other retailers who would compete with the prices offered by the Co-operative Society and offer credit which would be attractive to poorer families. (Credit was not part of the Rochdale model of co-operative retailing. It was offered by some societies but I have no evidence of its use in Chorley in this period). In 1871 a trade directory listed 123 shopkeepers and dealers in sundries in Chorley, excluding the Chorley Pilot Co-operative stores on the Market Place and at 58 Park Road.[370]

Co-operative shop prices for food and non-food goods were generally higher than those of private traders because of the need to make a greater profit per item in order to pay dividend. It has been shown that in many parts of Lancashire the local trader was successful in holding off the fierce competition of the new shops

---

[367] Firth Op. Cit. 28.
[368] *Chorley Standard* 7 April 1877.
[369] *Co-operative News* 10 February 1877.
[370] Slater's Directory 1871.

Co-operation in Chorley 1830-1880

because of their ability to meet the needs of the poorer sections of their local communities.[371] The Secretary of the Chorley Society referred to "very sharp competition …in Chorley, especially in Breadstuffs." [372]

Jim Heyes observed:

> For seven hundred years the market has been at the heart of Chorley's life, literally and metaphorically. The markets, traditionally held weekly on Tuesday and Saturday are one of the town's most enduring features.[373]

Thomas Gillibrand, the Lord of the Manor, had provided a market shed in the town centre in 1826.[374] The Improvement Commissioners in 1874 bought the market rights along with the manorial rights from the Fazakerley family. Fixed stalls started to appear on the market square. [375]In towns such as Chorley, Co-operative shops were beleaguered by "an association of private traders of every class (organised) to protect and promote their interests against ……..co-operative trading."[376]

Other shareholders invested in the society for financial reasons only. They were not primarily co-operators, although given the conservative ethos of Victorian Chorley they may have been also motivated by degrees of paternalism. This can be seen in the membership and support given by the Rigby family of Doctors, and millowners such as the Smethursts.

A typical invocation to members was given by Samuel Fairbrother when chairing a meeting in 1867:

> if they would bear in mind what he would tell them their dividend would be, instead of 1s 2d in

---

[371] Hodson, D. 1998. "The Municipal Store": Adaptation and Development in the Retail Markets of Nineteenth Century Urban Lancashire". Business History. 40/4. 94-114.
[372] *Chorley Standard* 17 February 1872.
[373] Heyes. Op. Cit. 99.
[374] Nattrass. Op. Cit..8.
[375] Ibid. 102.
[376] *Co-operative News* 20 October 1883.

the pound, considerably over. The Chairman then read a classification of the various articles which produced a large and moderate profit and those which scarcely produced profit at all, and strongly urged them to patronise their own establishment. It was not a wise policy to neglect their own interests in order to look after the interests of their friends. He deprecated the practice, and recommended the members in future to aid in the development of their own shop, where they could be as well supplied as by their friends, and it would be far more to their benefit, as they would receive a dividend on their expenditure.[377]

On other occasions, members were told that whilst dividends were low, so were prices when compared to other societies. Samuel Fairbrother, again as Chairman, suggested that some societies charged 20 to 30% more for their goods when compared to the prices of the Chorley Society.[378] However, just as Winstanley found high levels of dividend made membership "very attractive"[379], low levels of dividend not only would fail to attract new members, but did not offer a good reason for continued membership.

Level of dividend was a factor in the secession of Adlington members to form their own society in 1872. The loss of the Adlington members and business dealt a very severe blow to the Chorley Pilot Industrial Co-operative Society. Adlington lies midway between Chorley and Blackrod. In 1871 it was reported that whilst the Chorley Society was paying 1s 3d dividend, Blackrod was paying two shillings.[380]

Adlington had been an important part of the Chorley Society from its earliest days. The first report of a quarterly meeting of members mentions three elements of the receipts, Drapery £130 13s 2d, Groceries £2033 18s and Adlington branch £578 10s

---

[377] *Chorley Standard* 6 April 1867.
[378] Ibid. 4 April 1868
[379] Winstanley. Op. Cit. 38.
[380] *Chorley Standard* 7 January 1871.

Co-operation in Chorley 1830-1880

4d.[381] Members in Adlington had their own identity and had an Adlington Tea Party in the Temperance Hall in 1865.[382] Whilst the Society had other branches, the Adlington Branch was the oldest and almost certainly the most financially important. For example, when in 1866 a quarterly report highlighted Grocery sales, it showed that the Whittle branch's sales were £362, Crosse Hall's were £210 and Adlington's £655. (The Chorley store's grocery sales in that quarter were £3510).[383] Later that year, in recognition that the business in Adlington was expanding and the original store was too small and inaccessible for many residents, plans were agreed for a new store.[384] The belief was that if a central position could be found sales would grow further:

> In reply to Mr. W. Karfoot, the secretary (Mr. Hodgkinson) said they were at present paying a rent of £7 16s per year at Adlington and the sales had, during the last six month, nearly doubled those of the previous half year.- Mr. Critchley (Manager) remarked that he thought a new shop was very necessary; they were doing about £68 a week; the stock was much crammed, and the members were always asking how soon a new place was to be built. The shopman felt sure the sales would soon reach £100 per week, and was very anxious that a place should be built this summer.-A member said he had seen it himself, and thought it was very inconvenient.- The secretary observed that when they took it first, it was under a lease for five years, and this lease would expire in November, so it was a question for consideration whether the lease should be renewed. Mr. Critchley said that another objection to the present situation was that a large proportion of the members lived in Lower Adlington, and that was too far off. Mr. W. Karfoot

---

[381] *Preston Guardian* 4 January 1862.
[382] *Chorley Standard* 4 November 1865.
[383] *Preston Guardian* 6 January 1866.
[384] Ibid. 7 April 1866.

referred to a tea meeting, held at Adlington some time since, at which the matter was mooted and a lively interest in it was evinced by those who were present. It was not so much for them (the Chorley members) to find the money he thought, as to give them their patronage. He believed the sales would soon increase, if it were set a-going, and it would only require the efforts of the members at Adlington, whom he thought would raise sufficient funds amongst themselves to build it, so that it would not effect the funds much at Chorley, if that were any consideration. Mr. Critchley believed that that was so. Mr. Leach said the last time he was there the shopwoman told him she could do much more business in the drapery if she had more room.

It is interesting to note that the expectation was for the Adlington members to fund their own store. Whether this was the norm when branches were established in Crosse Hall, Brook Street, Park Road and Whittle is not known. It would certainly give the Adlington members a sense of "ownership" of their store.

The new store opened the following year, near to the Elephant and Castle Inn, at a cost of between £700 and £800 and a celebratory dinner was held .in Chorley![385] That notwithstanding, the new store was as successful as anticipated and the Society's Secretary reported almost a 50% increase in sales the following year.[386] The same year it was reported that several members from Adlington had attended a quarterly meeting. This must have been unusual. They asked for and were granted places on the Committee for Adlington members.[387]

There were no matters involving co-operation in Adlington reported until 1872 and the report in the *Chorley Standard* was headed "Secession of Adlington". This appeared to come "out of the blue", but the quarterly meeting's chairman said that Adlington members had been concerned about the low dividend and suspected

---

[385] *Chorley Standard* 7 September 1867.
[386] *The Co-operator* 14 March 1868
[387] *Chorley Standard* 4 July 1868.

that the Chorley part of the business pulled the dividend down. Other reasons put forward were higher prices in Adlington and "disunity" amongst the Chorley members. There was also a claim that when the Society had been formed, Adlington members had been promised to be allowed to go their own way "as soon as they had got enough".[388] Of the Adlington members canvassed, all but three were in favour of secession. From this point it appears that the secession was allowed to proceed on a reasonably amical basis. Premises and stock were sold for £1187.[389] Subsequent records of the Adlington Society show that 125 members transferred from Chorley. If it is optimistically assumed that the Chorley Society's membership had stayed at around the last known figure of 977 in 1868, it would have represented a loss of 12.8% of the members. Given the fall in sales from £29678 in 1868 to £25267 in 1871, it seems likely that membership had fallen, so Adlington's secession may have resulted in the loss of a fifth of the Chorley Society. By 1874 the Chorley Society's membership had fallen to 650.

The loss of Adlington Co-operators was possibly not just an issue to do with co-operation. There is a sense of Adlington asserting itself as a separate community. Residents petitioned the government in the same year for a Local Board of Health, again taking them out of the control of Chorley.[390] Whatever the reason, after Adlington's departure, the rump of the Chorley Pilot Industrial Co-operative Society was much diminished and never recovered its former size and strength.

Membership was down to 459 in 1878 when Withnell Industrial Co-operative Society had 259 members, Wheelton 124 in 1875 and Adlington 130 in 1880. (The respective populations in the 1871 census were Chorley 16,864. Withnell 1,966, Wheelton 1,471 and Adlington 2,606).

Arguably, in the second half of the 1870s, retail Co-operation was stronger in the villages to the north, east and west of Chorley than in Chorley itself. Clearly there would be less competition in those communities, but the Chorley Society struggled with the accumulated baggage of disputes between members, lack

---

[388] Ibid. 6 July 1872.
[389] Ibid. 9 November 1872.
[390] Ibid. 3 August 1872.

of stability and ability in day to day management, and the lack of patronage by half its members. Quarterly financial reports show a steady haemorrhaging of funds as members withdrawing funds regularly exceeded new capital by significant amounts. For example, in 1878 looking at four quarterly reports £51 was received in new contributions whilst £427 was withdrawn. By the end of 1878 the dividend was down to 6d.

The wider economic context was also a significant factor. In 1874 the long period of mid-Victorian prosperity was coming to an end. There was a major depression between 1877 and 1879, and as shown earlier that impacted on the industry of Chorley, including the Co-operative Mill. This depression caused severe hardship and reduced the spending ability of co-operative customers. That notwithstanding, the retail co-op contributed to the town's relief fund in 1879 (10 shillings and 100 loaves), whilst each of the leading millowners put in £5.

The demise of the retail society, with hindsight, might have appeared inevitable, but the active members and committee continued to look at ways of growing the business. In May 1879, public baking was offered in the bakehouse and this was advertised in the *Chorley Standard* each week until August. However, in July the dividend was down to 4d and a special meeting was called "for the purpose of considering the desirability of placing the working of the Society on a more economical footing".[391] It is not known what specifically led to the meeting being called or what resulted from that meeting, if it took place, but by October the dividend had dropped to 2d. This must have been very depressing for members and it reduced the advantages of shopping at the Co-op to a minimum. At the same time other local co-ops were known to be paying much higher dividends; Adlington 2 shillings in 1877, Heapey Busy Bee 2 shillings and sixpence in 1878, Wheelton two shillings and eightpence in 1876, White Coppice one shilling and sixpence in 1878 and Withnell 2 shillings and tuppence in 1879.

The Chorley Society staggered on and in 1880 witnessed conflicting fortunes in other neighbouring societies. The Wigan

---

[391] *Chorley Guardian* 5 July 1879.

and District Society was wound up in August,[392] having only been registered with the Co-operative Union in 1877.[393] On the other hand the Leyland and Farrington Society had a tea party that was such a success that many could not gain admittance.[394] It had been founded in the mid-1870s, and in 1879 paid a dividend of 2 shillings and 9d in the pound to its members.

In the same edition of the *Chorley Guardian* that reported the success of Leyland and Farrington, it reported on a special meeting of the Chorley Pilot Industrial Co-operative Society.[395] An audit had identified a deficiency of £1147. The manager and secretary denied responsibility. The auditors' report made grim reading as it identified sums not accounted for, corrections to the books, and other irregularities. The Chairman thought that the deficit had accumulated over a period of time. The Committee was accused of negligence by Mr. Rigby. This was probably the Justice, former general practitioner and landowner. He was brutally critical:

> Those who kept the books were to blame for the present state of matters, and the blame also rested with the committee, who must have been the most bloated dolts in the world to have allowed things to have gone on in the way they had. Although the society paid heavy wages to their salesmen, some of them abused the customers, while others of their number could not reckon up small amounts. On two occasions his housekeeper brought back money that ought to have been in the till, she not having been charged enough for her purchases. The committee could hardly fail to have been aware of the neglect that attended the institution.........
> It seems to me that any old woman would have managed the affairs of the Society better than the committee have done. It also seems to me that they were a self-elected body.

---

[392] Ibid. 28 August 1880
[393] 9TH Co-operative Congress 1877.
[394] *Chorley Guardian* 20 November 1880.
[395] Ibid.

John E. Harrison

The significance of the situation to ordinary members was expressed by Mr. Lloyd.

> Although he had not much in the Society, he had now lost a considerable amount. He thought it would be no use going on with the concern so long as the confidence had gone. It would be better to wind-up at once.

The motion to wind up the Society was moved by Mr. Carr, who claimed that he was "the first man to write his name for the society." (This was probably William Carr, a cotton weaver).

The motion was supported by the former Society Secretary Thomas Hodgkinson who said "Persons had been put in places who were not competent to fill them, and he did not think it would be wise to continue the Society longer." The motion was carried. The final comment by William Carr showed the degree of disillusionment:

> He believed that it was the impression of 95% of the members that the Society had been a swindle, and now they had determined that they would not again be swindled.

The following week the Park Road Branch store and its stock were put up for auction whilst the Market Place stores were advertised for sale by private treaty. Separately, four lots of three cottages "Cheap to Building Societies and others. Tenanted and in good repair" were advertised. These may well have also belonged to the retail co-operative.[396]

Co-operation in Chorley had failed, but regionally and nationally it was still growing. In 1881, when the first accurate figures were available, there were 971 societies, mainly in the north, with over half a million members.[397] Co-operation in Chorley revived in the year of Victoria's jubilee. A new Chorley Co-operative Society was formed on 7 August 1887, in part, its

---

[396] Ibid. 27 November 1880.
[397] Winstanley. Op. Cit. 37.

historian wrote, as "a momento of that occasion." It was not a totally celebratory occasion however as Longton reported that there was still plenty of ill-will following the loss of money in the old co-op by local shareholders.[398]

---

[398] Longton. Op. Cit. 11.

CONCLUSIONS

It is difficult to draw common conclusions about the experiences of the three businesses which tried to pursue the principles of Robert Owen and Co-operation, given that they operated in different eras and areas of business.

The Birkacre Co-operative was on the fringe of Chorley, taking advantage of a site and premises that had been in use for decades. It may well have been pure chance that the Blockprinter's Union acquired them. The Union, based in Manchester, had wanted to move into Co-operative Production and create a Co-operative community. It so happened that Birkacre was available. The stimulus to founding the Co-operative was largely external to Chorley, although almost certainly supported by local print workers. The plans were ambitious, capital was limited, members may have disagreed, the quality of the product may have been variable, but the collapse of the business may well have been due to trading conditions of the times, rather than its Co-operative structure and goals.

By the 1860s, as Pollard pointed out

> the speedy collapse of capitalism was no longer expected .... the task of working class organisations was merely to establish the best possible positions within it.[399]

---

[399] Pollard, Sidney, 1960. Nineteenth-Century Co-operation: From Community Building to Shopkeeping in Essays in Labour History edited by Briggs, Asa and Saville, John. London. 108.

Ambition was not in short supply for either the Chorley Co-operative Mill or the Pilot Retail Society. The founders of the mill were Co-operators and had leased a large area of land and clearly hoped to move from weaving into spinning, to provide houses and possibly more. In its relatively short life, it certainly increased its weaving capacity. Similarly, the retail society had great ambitions for the business and expanded departments and branches as well as building the Co-operative Hall, baths and a library and reading room.

The lack of capital for the Co-operative Mill, meant that many of its ambitions were unfulfilled and ultimately left it vulnerable to one of the worst trade depressions of the nineteenth century. However, the shortfall between actual capital and aimed for capital did not prevent the company from operating successfully and paying dividends to shareholders for more than a decade. The management of the business came in for criticism from trade unions and its workers, but by the standards of the nineteenth century it must be judged to have been quite successful. Labour relations by the late 1870s were clearly poor, but it was almost certainly the trade depression that brought the Co-operative Mill to its knees like many other businesses across Lancashire. Whether it was truly a co-operative business is an issue for academic argument. However, I am satisfied that it was founded by co-operators who lacked a template on which to model it. By the time of its collapse, it was clearly only co-operative in name.

Capital was less of an issue for the retail society and only became a problem towards the end of its life as members lost confidence and withdrew their capital. Factionalism was certainly a factor in the Pilot Society's failure. This was particularly illustrated with the conflict between teetotallers and others, but as the business entered more testing times there was much evidence of disagreements between and amongst members, officers, committee members and supporters. The fact that Chorley was a market town also meant that there was strong competition in the retail sector, making it difficult for the Pilot Society to hold onto its market share in times of economic downturns. Longton had written that the promoters and officials lacked the business ability, knowledge, or training necessary to make a permanent success of their undertaking.[400]

The phrase has always seemed a sweeping damnation, particularly given the success of the business in its first decade. How many retail businesses in Chorley in the 1860s were run by people who had knowledge, training and proven ability? The answer must be "Precious few!" However, once the Society lost its first Secretary and Manager, it seemed to lose a degree of stability, and although the Karfoots continued to provide support, it may well have lacked managers of sufficient experience and quality to steer the business through the crises of the 1870s.

Criticism can be made of the "apathy" of society members. Gurney says such criticism was warranted and that it was a "constant source of complaint."[401] It would appear that at most quarterly meetings of the Chorley Pilot Society, attendance was low. Whether this should be described as apathetic is debatable. It could be argued that meetings were held in the evenings after long and hard-working days, and that in periods where it appeared the Society was prospering and running well, there appeared less need to attend. In Chorley members were criticised for not patronising the business rather than not attending meetings.

Political support, or the lack of it, was a feature that at this time may have been a factor in the failure of the mill and the retail society to survive. Firth emphasised the importance of the support of Liberal politicians, particularly in Burnley in encouraging the growth and prosperity of the co-operative movement in the Borough.[402] Chorley was not a Liberal town. It had Liberal figures, such as the co-operator William Karfoot and millowner William Lawrence, but it was largely conservative politically.

Pennine-bordering communities where co-operation took an early and strong hold were also characterised by being strongly non-conformist. Chorley was not. It had a number of non-conformist

---

[400] Longton. Op.Cit. 10.
[401] Gurney. Op. Cit. 49.
[402] Firth. Op. Cit. 77.

churches and chapels, but it had a strong Anglican tradition with a substantial Catholic community. I have not found evidence of any religious negativity towards co-operation in the town, but clearly the non-conformist base to build upon was smaller and less substantial.

The pen pictures of the Co-operators in Chorley in the period 1860-80 are incomplete. Firth's conclusions from looking at the clientele of North East Lancashire Co-operatives was clear. They were weavers. Spinners and others in "subordinate" jobs in the mills did not even play a minor role in the local co-operative movement[403]. I cannot be so categoric in writing about Chorley. Weavers (Handloom and power loom) were certainly major players in the founding of the Co-operative Mill (it was a weaving business after all!) and the retail society, and as can be seen from the appendix, played important roles in the village co-operatives in the area. However, spinners and other textile workers were shareholders in the mill and given the diversity of industry and textile businesses in the town, are likely to have participated in the retail society as it grew to its peak membership of 1000.

Clearly the story of these three co-operative-inspired ventures in Chorley, was ultimately one of failure. However, there were positives. The Chorley Pilot Industrial Society, and also the other local village societies, mainly sold groceries. The aim of co-operation, particularly in the 1860s and 1870s when adulteration was rife, was to sell pure food and this was to the benefit of every member family when they bought their flour, butter, cheese, tea and bread. In addition, we should not overlook the success of working men and women coming together to raise capital, found businesses and run them successfully for periods of time. They were untrained, with limited education and needed guidance from other co-operators and co-operative businesses, but they provided foundations of belief in the Co-operative way of working which would be later successfully built upon by the Chorley Co-operative Society.

---

[403] Firth Op. Cit. 47.

APPENDIX

Co-operatives in Surrounding Townships 1860-80

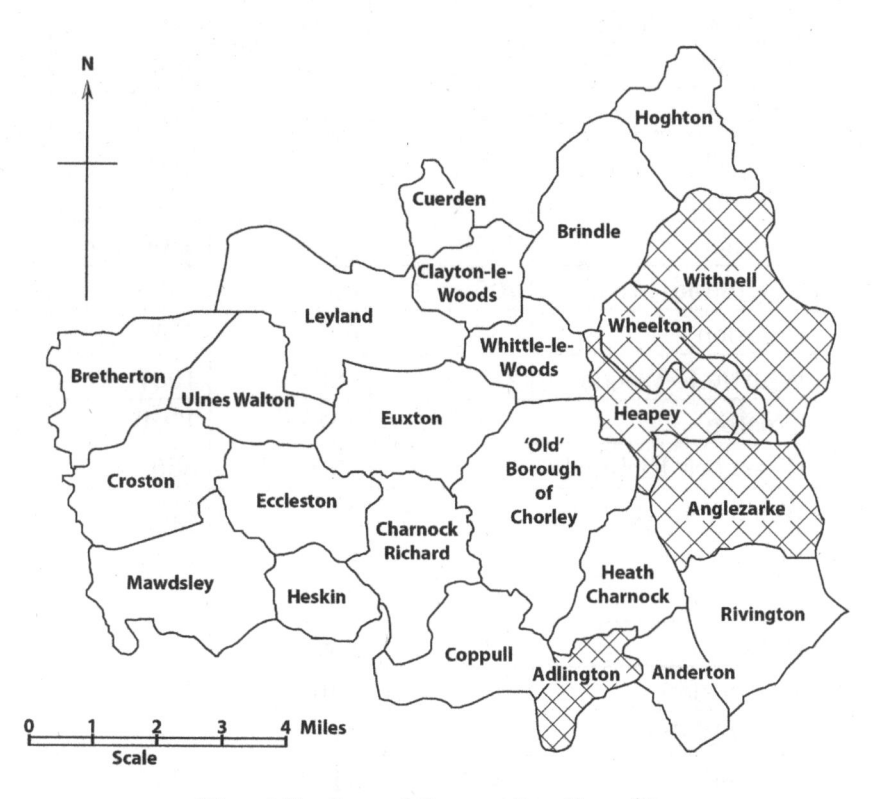

Map of Chorley and Surrounding Townships

Census returns for Chorley and Surrounding Townships 1861-1881

	1861	1871	1881
Chorley	15013	16864	19478
Coppull	1230	1484	1826
Duxbury	341	325	323
Heapey	396	290	369
Rivington	369	531	330
Adlington	1975	2606	3258
Anderton	243	262	317
Anglezarke	134	195	99
Heath Charnock	772	1034	916
Leyland	3755	3839	4961
Brindle	1501	1339	1173
Hoghton	1201	906	871
Wheelton	1260	1471	1570
Withnell	2059	1966	2106
Clayton-le-Woods	705	607	582
Cuerdon	666	647	573
Whittle-le-Woods	2151	1805	1937
Croston	1790	1518	1791
Charnock Richard	899	750	685
Welch Whittle	148	111	115
Bretherton	775	683	707
Eccleston	965	953	900
Heskin	439	336	382
Mawdesley	912	886	928
Ulnes Walton	488	414	386
Euxton	1491	1182	1147

Information about Co-operatives in the communities around Chorley in the period when the Chorley Pilot Industrial Co-operative Society was operating is thin. Few Society records have survived and the National Co-operative publications and the Chorley newspapers do not report these Societies as frequently as the Chorley Society, or in as much detail. That notwithstanding, the brief histories which follow show that on a much smaller scale, these village co-operatives had a different history and survived the troubled economic years of the second half of the 1870s. Nevertheless, from what is known of membership figures at this time, they remained small, and this is similar to Firth's findings in North East Lancashire[404]

Adlington Industrial Co-operative Society

The early years of Co-operation in Adlington when it was under the aegis of the Chorley Pilot Industrial Co-operative Society were described in Chapter 3, and the secession from Chorley was described in Chapter 7. The first quarterly meeting of the new Adlington Industrial Co-operative Society was reported in the *Chorley Guardian* on the 11th January 1873. A profit of £181 was made in the first quarter and members received a dividend of 1s 8d.[405] 125 members had transferred from the Chorley Society and by September 1873 membership had grown to 188.[406]

In membership terms the Society remained at a similar level for a few years although a report in 1877 gives an indication of some difficulties with reference to "better management" and "members seemed to have more confidence in the Society than had been shown for some time past". Dividend paid was 2s in the pound, possibly the highest it had been since the Society had been formed and higher than under the Chorley Society[407]. Nevertheless, at the same time that the Chorley Society was entering its final crisis, the economic depression was also hitting the Adlington Society as membership in 1880 was down to 130,

---

[404] Firth. Op. Cit. 7.
[405] *Chorley Guardian* 11 January 1873.
[406] Adlington Industrial Co-operative Society Records.
[407] *Chorley Standard* 6 October 1877

little better than when Adlington seceded from Chorley Pilot Industrial Co-operative Society.

Whilst very little is known about the individual early co-operators in the Chorley district it is remarkable that an obituary for an Adlington Co-operator was published in the *Co-operative News* in 1872. He was James Slater, an overlooker at a cotton mill. He was of "an ardent nature", and despite having been ill for several months, addressed a co-operative meeting in Adlington on the night before he died. His brother wrote:

> He was a co-operator to the backbone. He believed co-operation was the lever which should raise the working people of this country to that degree of comfort which they ought to occupy, considering the part they take in the creation of its wealth.

The obituary writer stated that to men such as James Slater "Co-operation owes its vitality, its progress, almost its existence."[408]

Leyland and Farrington Co-operative Society

Modern Leyland is a substantial town that has lost its ties to Chorley having experienced industrial growth in a later phase. However, it was in the nineteenth century part of the Chorley Poor Law Union and the second largest community within it, behind Chorley. The Leyland and Farrington Co-operative Society appears to have been formed in 1875. 700 shares had been taken up by ninety-five members and large premises obtained on Golden Hill. There were no other co-operatives in Leyland and Farrington so the business was expected to be successful.[409] By 1877, membership had reached 238, quarterly profit was £176 and dividend paid to members was 2s in the pound.[410] By 1879, this society was paying dividend of 2s 9d.

---

[408] *Co-operative News* 27 April 1872.
[409] *Chorley Standard* 3 July 1875.
[410] Ibid. 13 January 1877.

Withnell Co-operative Society.

The Withnell Society was founded in 1861, the year after the Chorley Pilot Industrial Co-operative Society. By the time it held its fourth quarterly meeting in 1862, it had forty-three members who had invested £140 3s 6d and was paying a dividend of 1s 6d.[411] The parish was largely rural but industrialisation had taken hold in the village as well as in Brinscall, Abbey Village and Withnell Fold. In addition, there was a history of handloom weaving. The reliance on industrial employment made workers vulnerable to the variables of the economic cycle and in 1863, as the Cotton Famine hit this community and other Lancashire communities, William Cartmell, the Society Secretary reported that distress was bitterly felt, but "Co-operation is the silver lining to our cloud of distress".[412] Cartmell was a thirty-two year old warehouseman in the 1861 census who had been born in Blackburn. He clearly had some standing as a Co-operator in the area as he was one of the speakers at the opening of the Co-operative Hall in Chorley in 1864.

William Cartmell moved back to Blackburn and seems to have been replaced as Secretary by H B Backhouse who worked at the Withnell Fold Paper Mill. The other important figure in the Society in its first decade was Jesse Butterfield, a Fent Dealer. He would seem to have been something of a character as at the Annual Tea Meeting in 1867, after the completion of formal business and "songs and glees were given", he sang a song called "The Blackburn, Chorley and Wigan Railway" which he had composed himself.[413]

Eighty people attended the 1867 Annual Tea Meeting, which would be largely made up of members and their family members. The dividend was reported to be 1s in the pound, which was a significantly lower figure than that reported above in 1862. However, it was reported that "considering the state of trade in the district, the prospects of the society are very encouraging".[414]

---

[411] *The Co-operator* August 1862.
[412] Ibid. January 1863
[413] *Chorley Standard* 5 January 1867.
[414] Ibid.

As mentioned before, reports by Co-operative societies rarely failed to be optimistic, however this report seems to have been justified as by October in the same year, forty-nine members were being paid a dividend of 2s 2d. The Secretary, H B Backhouse, reminded members that

> the dividend at the quarter's end is not the only thing to be obtained, but that it is designed to raise the working classes, socially, morally and intellectually.[415]

The following month the new Co-operative store was opened and 150 people had a celebratory tea.[416]

An upward curve was maintained in terms of membership. There were ninety in 1871[417] and 140 in 1874, when trade was in Grocery, Provisions and Drapery.[418] By 1876 membership had reached 271, quarterly cash receipts were £3,647 and the dividend was 2s 3d. The Society had also established a Penny Savings Bank for members' children and the wider public.[419]

The membership figure of 1876 was the highpoint of the decade as there was a small dip to 259 in 1878, reflecting the national economic depression of the latter part of the decade. That notwithstanding, dividend remained at a level that Chorley Co-operative members could only dream of, being 2s 4d in 1877 and 2s 2d in 1880. Given the crisis experienced by the Chorley Pilot Industrial Co-operative Society in 1868 in its Drapery Department, it is interesting to note that the Withnell Society had to allow £10 for depreciation of drapery in 1877.[420] This was presumably stock that could not be sold or could not be sold at the expected price. However, this would seem to be a minor hiccup in a success story. By 1890, it had branches in Abbey Village and

---

[415] Ibid. 12 October 1867.
[416] Ibid. 9 November 1867.
[417] Co-operative Congress Statistical Return
[418] Co-operative Handbook 1874.
[419] *Chorley Standard* 15 July 1876.
[420] Ibid. 14 July 1877.

Brinscall, as well as the Withnell shop and in 1911 it celebrated its Jubilee with a commemorative plate.

Detail from plate celebrating 50 years of the Withnell Industrial Co-operative Society

White Coppice Co-operative Society

White Coppice is largely in Anglezarke township and had a weaving shed belonging to Alfred Ephraim Eccles, a leading abstainer and supporter of the Temperance Movement. Eccles was a patriarchal figure, a Liberal and reformer. He retired from business at the age of forty-three in around 1873 to focus on the advancement of temperance. As well as providing housing for his workers, he and his wife "looked well after the people of White Coppice, taking care that there should be no temptation to waste or bad habits".[421] His boast was that White Coppice was the only township in the United Kingdom without a beer shop. Instead he provided a newsroom, The Band of Hope, a Sunday School and Meeting Room, and a co-operative shop. The shop was at one end

---

[421] Anon. Life and Labour of AE Eccles. Chorley. 1909. 36.

of the mill building. Ernest Ashton was the Co-operative Society Secretary and John Smith was the manager.[422]

The Co-operative Society seems to have been founded in the mid-1870s. In 1878, at a Tea Party, the Secretary described it as "flourishing" and said members were paid a dividend of 1s 6d. It was clearly integrated into the area co-operative community as speeches were given by Thomas Hodgkinson, the former secretary of the Chorley Pilot Industrial Co-operative Society (and a supporter of Temperance).[423] An 1890 Directory listed the White Coppice Co-operative Stores under Grocers and General Dealers. There are no known membership figures for this Society at this time, but given that the 1881 census records the population of Anglezarke as being ninety-nine, it must have been small. In many ways White Coppice at this time could be seen as having similarities with Robert Owen's much larger community at New Lanark and with the plans for Birkacre earlier in the century. However, it is not known to what extent workers and co-operative members had control over their lives. Given what is known about A E Eccles, he would seem to have been not only paternalistic but also authoritarian.

The Wheelton Prospect Industrial Co-operative Society and the Heapey Busy Bee Co-operative Society.

The parishes of Heapey and Wheelton are so closely aligned that it is not surprising to find their experience of Co-operation to be also closely connected. The Wheelton Society was founded in November 1866

> by 13 working men, in a district thinly populated, with a capital of £50. It's first business was transacted in a cottage taken for the purpose.[424]

---

[422] Birtill, George, 1966. <u>The Enchanted Hills</u>. Chorley. 35.
[423] *Chorley Standard* 23 February 1878.
[424] *The Co-operator and Herald of Health* 23 January 1869.

By 1869 cottage property to the value of £600 had been bought and the Society's capital was valued at £812. Dividend to members was averaging 1s 6d in the pound.[425]

It seems that the Society was founded in Wheelton Stocks, now known as Higher Wheelton, as there was a shop was at the end of Bennett Row which may well have been the original shop. This was 100 metres from Crook Row, a row of Handloom Weavers' Cottages with cellar loomshops. Other handloom weavers' cottages have been identified further along the road, so it seems likely that weavers from this community were important in the foundation of this society.[426] Equally important were papermakers from the paper mill in Withnell Fold and the Secretary was a paper mill worker. Cotton was also spun in Wheelton Stocks at Sitch Mill, behind the Golden Lion pub, so textile mill workers may also have been involved with the Society. Many of the original members of the Society may well have been non conformists as a Wesleyan Chapel was built in Wheelton Stocks in 1842 and a Methodist Chapel in Withnell Fold in 1852. There were no other places of worship in Wheelton at this time.

The Secretary, who submitted the report to *The Co-operator*, was William Blacklidge, described in the 1861 census as a wheelwright and in 1871 as a Paper Maker Machine Man. Like H B Backhouse, the Secretary of the Withnell Society, he would have been employed at the Withnell Fold Paper Mill, which was barely a kilometre from the site of the Wheelton Society's first shop.

From small beginnings, the Society grew steadily. The first AGM in 1868 was told that annual receipts were in excess of £1200, profits £142 and dividends averaged 1s 3d. It was decided that the present place of business was too small and that a new shop and two cottage houses be built. In addition, 280 shares were enrolled, to be paid up when called for.[427] Given the relatively small membership and similar local population, it must have been

---

[425] Ibid.
[426] Timmins, J. G., 1977. <u>Handloom Weavers' Cottages in Central Lancashire</u>. Occasional Paper No.3. Centre for North West Regional Studies, University of Lancaster. 68.
[427] *Chorley Standard* 11 January 1868.

expected that there would be multiple share ownership within families.

The following year's AGM was similarly "upbeat" with growth reported allowing an average dividend of 1s 8d and the employment of a shopman. The society was also paying for "carriage" which presumably indicated that previously members had travelled to obtain and buy goods to be sold in the shop. Membership stood at sixty-three with, over the year, eighteen new members and three withdrawals[428].

As seen with other local societies Tea Meetings were held to promote Co-operation in the wider community and reward existing members and their families. The Wheelton Society held a tea meeting early in 1869 at the Brown Cow Inn in Wheelton. (The location may indicate a lack of temperance influence in the Society, but equally it may indicate a lack of alternative meeting places as 120 members and friends attended.) William Karfoot, the Chorley Co-operator, chaired the meeting and spoke "at considerable length on co-operation, the benefits and advantages, its friends and enemies." One of the members, Thomas Brindle, described as a Handloom Weaver in the 1861 census, described the Society's beginnings in late 1866 "under very gloomy circumstances" but had developed "through the zealous self-sacrifice of its committees". Through the influence of the Society:

> Members were taught to pay ready money and led to see the wisdom of abolishing that penny-wise and pound-foolish system of badge books and long credit.[429]

Annual reports continued to show growth. In 1872 Dividend was 2s in the pound and membership seventy-one[430] and in 1873 dividend was 2s 4d and membership reached eighty. In the latter year it was decided that because their present premises were too small "and the great inconvenience experienced in the warehousing of goods" the Society would build a new store on

---

[428] Ibid. 9 January 1869.
[429] Ibid. 13 February 1869.
[430] Ibid. 6 January 1872.

the Society's own land."[431] Clearly the Society had outgrown the use of cottages. By the time of the 1874 AGM, the new premises were approaching completion and the total capital of the society exceeded £1033[432]. Incomplete newspaper reporting means that as yet there is little information about the new store. However, it was open by September 1875 when the thirty fifth quarterly meeting was held in the "large room at the stores"[433]. The annual meeting held four months later referred to "the No.1 branch just opened at Lower Lane.[434]"

Lower Lane was the name used for the area now known as Wheelton. This was a significant re-location for the business and it reflects the industrial changes over the past decade with the decline of handloom weaving and the growth of factory-based textile production. A spinning and weaving mill had been built in Lower Lane on the border of the Wheelton and Heapey communities by Peter Todd in 1859. The mill produced gold thread and the building and subsequent expansion of the mill caused most of the present village to be built, and the Wheelton population to grow from 1041 in 1851 to 1570 in 1881. Three new streets were built specifically for the mill workers.

The quarterly meeting in 1875 was the earliest reference found where the business was referred to as the Wheelton Prospect Co-operative Stores. The millowner, Peter Todd, lived at Prospect House, which he had built in 1864, so it is reasonable to assume that the addition of Prospect in the Society's name was an acknowledgement of the millowner's support (or the support of his family, given that Todd died in 1874), perhaps in the provision of land for the new shop. Barnes described Peter Todd as being "paternalistic to a fault".[435] Although the Lower Lane store was referred to as the No 1 store the Bennett Row shop was still seen

---

[431] Ibid. 11 January 1873
[432] Ibid. 3 January 1874.
[433] Ibid. 25 September 1875.
[434] Ibid. 22 January 1876.
[435] Barnes, Roger, 2010. "He rejoiced to see them comfortable"? The impact of Peter Todd on the Lower Lane Community of Wheeleton, Lancashire. 1841-1881. Witney. Vi.

as the base in an 1878 Co-operative Directory[436]. Confusingly, an 1890 Directory, non-Co-operative, has the Wheelton Co-operative Society as Grocers and General Dealers and the Wheelton Prospect Society listed under Linen Drapers. I think this was an error and there were two stores, part of the same business[437].

However, by 1876 there was a new Co-operative in name in Lower Lane. This was the Heapey Busy Bee Co-operative. It was registered on 7 June 1876[438]. I do not believe there were two Co-operative businesses in Lower Lane. The Heapey Society was a breakaway from the Wheelton Society. A quarterly report in 1880 refers the Society starting "on its own footing" in June 1876[439]. The Wheelton Society's membership fell from 124 in January 1876[440] to eighty members in 1877[441]. The breakaway may well have much to do with the Todds. Peter Todd was a man of strong views. In 1868 he was Churchwarden at St. Barnabas, Heapey and had a bitter dispute with the Vicar. Todd and his followers, mainly employees, broke away and formed their own Free Church of England, building their own St. Peter's Church and School in Wheelton[442]. A "voluntary" subscription funded the new premises, but it seems that workers had little choice than to pay. Todd had died in 1874, but the business had passed to the Jackson family through Todd's only child, his daughter Margaret.

There is no evidence as to why the split occurred. It may have been that the millowner wanted a separate organisation which could be controlled more easily, but it may well reflect the different industrial communities served by the Society. Lower Lane served the employees of the Todd's Victoria Mill whereas Bennett's Row shop served the employees of Sitch Mill, at least until it was almost completely destroyed by fire in 1885, the dwindling handloom weaver community and employees of the

---

[436] Co-operative Directory 1878 issued by the Central Co-operative Board.
[437] Slater's Directory 1890.
[438] 9TH Co-operative Congress 1877.
[439] *Chorley Guardian* 3 January 1880.
[440] *Chorley Standard* 22 January 1876.
[441] Co-operative Directory. Op. Cit.
[442] Hodgkinson, Kenneth, 1987. Heapey and District, A Pictorial Record of Bygone Days. Chorley. 28.

Parke's Withnell Fold Paper Mill. The latter connection had been important since the Society's foundation, was maintained through William Blacklidge, Secretary of the Society and employee of the Paper Mill, and in the 1890's the Wheelton Society took over the management of the existing grocer's shop in Withnell Fold.

The Heapey Busy Bee Co-operative Society would appear to have started with around forty members, that being the difference between the Wheelton Society's membership in 1876 and 1877. It grew rapidly from this base, having ninety-six members in 1877[443]. It's quarterly sales figures in April 1878 were over £900[444], whereas the Wheelton Society's sales for the whole of 1875 had only amounted to £2,800[445]. There was no noticeable gain to members in terms of dividend (an issue for Adlington members in the secession from the Chorley Pilot Industrial Society). Wheelton paid an average of 2s 8d in 1875[446], Heapey paid 2s 6d in 1878[447] and again in 1880.[448]

Barnes suggested that the arrival of a Co-operative business in Lower Lane may have been delayed by Peter Todd in order to protect the grocer's business of his brother-in-law Edward Williams in Victoria Street.[449] This is certainly a possibility.

Whittle le Woods Star Co-operative Society

Co-operative retailing seems to have been introduced to Whittle le Woods by the Chorley Pilot Industrial Co-operative Society. In 1865 the Society looked into opening branches in Euxton and in Whittle le Woods. The Euxton project was put on hold, and evidently did not proceed, because a local mill was having a difficult time. There was greater support for a branch at Whittle. Mr. M. Karfoot moved

---

[443] Co-operative Directory. Op. Cit.
[444] *Chorley Standard* 6 April 1878.
[445] Ibid. 22 January 1876.
[446] Ibid. 22 January 1876.
[447] Ibid. 6 April 1878.
[448] *Chorley Guardian* 3 April 1880.
[449] Barnes. Op. Cit. 43.

That the Committee make investigation to see whether it would be advantageous to open a branch store in Whittle le Woods, and that they have the power to open one in case they find it will be advantageous.[450]

In a quarterly report at the start of 1866, the Chorley Society reported on sales at branches in Adlington, Crosse Hall and Whittle. Sales in the past quarter at Whittle had been £362, half of the Adlington sales but £150 better than Crosse Hall[451]. However later in the year, profits at Whittle appeared to be negligible and "It was the opinion of the directors that the store had been grossly neglected, and a thorough investigation must be made."[452] Within two and a half years the branch had been given up[453]. No reason for the closure was given, but 1868 had been a difficult year for the Chorley Society with losses in the Drapery Department, so the Whittle branch may well have been closed as part of a strategy to concentrate business in the core Adlington and Chorley branches.

The Star Co-operative Society would seem to have been formed as a consequence of this closure by Whittle residents intent on maintaining a Co-operative business. A Tea Meeting held early in 1869 may have been a launch event. It was attended by "about eighty of the members and their families." There was clearly still a good relationship with the Chorley Society as Thomas Hodgkinson, the Chorley Secretary chaired and addressed the meeting and a later speech was given by William Karfoot. The other major speech was given by Henry Bolton of Whittle. He had been born in Withnell and seems to have been a handloom weaver in the 1861 census. Whether Henry Bolton's occupation was typical of the Whittle Star membership is not known. There certainly were handloom weavers in the village[454], however there

---

[450] *Chorley Standard* 19 August 1865.
[451] *Preston Guardian* 6 January 1866.
[452] *Chorley Standard* 7 July 1866.
[453] Ibid 4 July 1868.
[454] Timmins Op, Cit. 74.

was also employment in brewing, sandstone quarries and in bleaching and dyeing at Lower Kem Mill.

The Whittle Star Co-operative was not reported upon in the Chorley newspapers and records do not survive. It would seem to have prospered however as by 1904 it had 205 members.

BIBLIOGRAPHY

1. Archival Sources

   - Adlington Industrial Co-operative Society Records
   - Baines Lancashire Directory Vol. 1 1824.
   - Burgh Hall Sale Documents 1901. Lancashire County Record Office DDHH 1/139 31 July 1901
   - Butterworth Edwin. A Statistical Sketch of the County Palatine of Lancaster 1841. Manchester.
   - Chorley Co-operative Spinning and Weaving Co. Ltd. National Archives BT 31/559/2282.
   - Chorley Tithe Map. Lancashire County Record Office DRB 1/43
   - Chorley Valuation 1871 Lancashire County Record Office MBCH 36/3.
   - Co-operative Congress Reports and Papers
   - Co-operative Directory 1878.
   - Co-operative Handbook 1874.
   - Graham J. The Chemistry of Calico Printing and History of Printworks in the Manchester District from 1760-1846. (Manchester Central Reference Library).
   - Greenfield Mill (1914) Plan attached to Conveyance of Albert Mills and Primrose Bank Weaving Shed by George Thomas Brown to George Brown (Chorley) Limited. Chorley Heritage Society.
   - Letter to Robert Owen from Mr. Carson of Haigh. 1st March 1832. Letter 522 in Robert Owen's Correspondence.

- London Working Mens Association. Journal of Association. 1852
- Mannex P and Co. Topography and Directory of Mid Lancashire. Beverley. 1851
- Organization of Labour: Report of Committee appointed 6th September 1851 to consider and devise the best method of carrying out the Block-Printers' desire of Trades' Co-operation into effect. Paisley 1851.
- James Pigot and Co. New Commercial Directory for the Counties of Cheshire, Derbyshire and Lancashire. Manchester. 1830.
- Robinson C. An Historical and Descriptive Account of Chorley. Chorley 1835.
- The Charter.
- Slater's Directory 1871.
- Slater's Directory 1890
- Universal British Directory 1793-1798. Vol.2 Part 2.

2. Newspapers and Periodicals

- Bolton Chronicle.
- Bury and Norwich Post
- Cobbett's Weekly Political Register
- Chorley Standard
- Chorley Guardian
- Co-operative News
- House of Commons Journal XXXVII
- Lancaster Gazetter
- Manchester Mercury
- Manchester Times and Gazette
- Preston Chronicle
- Preston Guardian
- Preston Pilot
- The Era
- The Christian Socialist
- The Co-operator
- The Co-operator and Herald of Health
- The Crisis

- The Lancashire Co-operator
- The Lancashire and Yorkshire Co-operator
- The Times Digital Archive.

3. Published Works, Theses, Papers etc

- Anon. Life and Labour of A E Eccles. Chorley. 1909.
- Ashmore O (1969). Industrial Archaeology of Lancashire. Newton Abbot. David and Charles.
- Barnes R (2010). "He rejoiced to see them comfortable"? The impact of Peter Todd on the Lower Lane community of Wheelton, Lancashire. 1841-1881. Witney. Privately published.
- Baron M (1998). Victorian Shopping. London. Michael O'Mara Books.
- Bee M (1997). Industrial Revolution and Social Reform in the Manchester Region. Manchester. Neil Richardson.
- Benson J and Shaw G (1992). The Evolution of Retail Systems c1800-1914. Leicester. Leicester University Press.
- Bibby A (2015). All Our Own Work. The Co-operative Pioneers of Hebden Bridge and their mill. London. Merlin Press.
- Birchall J (1994). Co-op. The People's Business. Manchester. Manchester University Press.
- Birtill G (1966), The Enchanted Hills. Chorley. Guardian Press.
- Chesters A (2006) "Working Class Limiteds: Co-operative Cotton Companies in S. E. Lancashire, 1850-1880. Unpublished MA Dissertation Lancaster.
- Cole G D H (1944). A Century of Co-operation. London. Allen and Unwin.
- Cole G D H and Postgate R (1938). The Common People. London. Methuen.
- Cole J. (1994). Conflict and Co-operation. Rochdale and the Pioneering Spirit. 1790-1844. Littleborough. George Kelsall.
- Cummings, Edward. "Co-Operative Production in France and England." *The Quarterly Journal of Economics*,

vol. 4, no. 4, 1890, pp. 357–386. *JSTOR*, www.jstor.org/stable/1881742.
- Everitt J (1997). Co-operative Society Libraries and Newsrooms of Lancashire and Yorkshire from 1844 to 1918. Unpublished D. Phil. Thesis. University of Wales, Aberystwyth.
- Farnie, D (1979). The English Cotton Industry and the World Market. Oxford. Clarendon Press.
- Firth P (1991). The Co-operative Movement and the Working Class in North East Lancashire 1870-1914.
- Fitton R S (1989). The Arkwrights. Spinners of Fortune. Manchester. Manchester University Press.
- Garnett R G (1972). Co-operation and the Owenite socialist communities in Britain, 1825-45. Manchester. Manchester University Press.
- Gurney P (1996). Co-operative Culture and the Politics of Consumption in England 1870-1930. Manchester. Manchester University Press.
- Hampson P (2011) Working Class Capitalism in Victorian Lancashire in Bulletin of Local and Family History. Vol. 4.
- Hampson P W (February 2015). Working Class Capitalists. The development and financing of worker-owned companies, in the Irwell Valley, 1849-1875. Unpublished Phd. Thesis. University of Central Lancashire.
- Harrison J (2010). Campaign for Public Baths in Victorian Chorley in Lancashire Quarterly History. Vol. 13 No1.
- Harrison J E (1983). The Development of Medical Care and Public Health in Nineteenth Century Chorley. Unpublished MSc Thesis. University of Manchester.
- Harrison J F C. (1969). Robert Owen and the Owenites in Britain and America-The Quest for the New Moral World. London. Routledge.
- Heyes J (1994). A History of Chorley. Preston. Lancashire County Books.
- Hobsbawm E J (1968) Industry and Empire. London. Pelican.
- Hodgkinson K (1987), Heapey and District, A Pictorial Record of Bygone Days. Chorley. C K D Publications.

- Hodson D (1998). The Municipal Store: Adaptation and Development in the Retail Markets of Nineteenth Century Urban Lancashire". Business History.
- Holyoake G J (1857). Self Help by the People: The History of the Rochdale Pioneers. London. Allen and Unwin.
- Holyoake G J (1875). The History of Co-operation in England, its Literature, and its Advocates Vol. 1. London. Fisher Unwin.
- Hunt D (1997). A History of Walton- le-Dale and Bamber Bridge. Lancaster. Carnegie.
- Jones B. (1894) Co-operative Production. Oxford. Clarendon Press.
- King J E (1981). Richard Marsden and the Preston Chartists 1837-1848. Lancaster. Lancaster University.
- Kirby R G and Musson A E (1975). The Voice of the People. John Doherty, 1798-1854. Trade Unionist, Radical and Factory Reformer. Manchester. Manchester University Press.
- Longton F (1937). Fifty Years of Co-operation in Chorley. 1887-1937. Chorley Co-operative Society Limited.
- Marshall J D (1974). Lancashire. Newton Abbot. David and Charles.
- Morgan C E (1992) Work and Consciousness in the Mid-Nineteenth-Century English Cotton Industry in Social History, Vol.17. No1. January 1992.
- Musson A E (1972). British Trade Unions 1800-1875. London. Macmillan.
- Musson A E (1974). Trade Union and Social History. London. Frank Cass.
- Nattrass L B (1974). The Governing Elite in Chorley, 1854-1914. Lancaster. Unpublished MA Dissertation.
- Pollard S (1960) Nineteenth Century Co-operation: From Community Building to Shopkeeping in Essays in Labour History edited by Briggs A and Saville J. London. Macmillan.
- Pollard S and Salt J. (1971) Robert Owen: Prophet of the Poor. Lewisburg.

- Potter B (1891). The Co-operative Movement in Great Britain. London. Geo. Unwin and Unwin.
- Sykes R (1982). Early Chartism and Trade Unionism in South-East Lancashire in The Chartist Experience, Studies in Working Class Radicalism and Culture, 1830-1860 edited by Epstein J and Thompson D. London. Macmillan.
- Taylor J C. (1900). The Jubilee History of the Oldham Industrial Co-operative Society Limited. Manchester. Co-operative Wholesale Society.
- Thompson E P (1970). The Making of the English Working Class. London. Penguin.
- Timmins J G (1977). Handloom Weavers' Cottages in Central Lancashire. Occasional Paper No.3. Centre for North West Regional Studies, University of Lancaster.
- Toms S (2007). Oldham Capitalism and the Rise of the Lancashire Textile Industry. Working Paper number 30. University of York.
- Turnbull J and Southern J (1995). More Than Just a Shop. A History of the Co-op in Lancashire. Lancashire County Books.
- Turner H A (1962) Trade Union Growth, Structure and Policy- A Comparative Study of the Cotton Unions. London. Allen and Unwin.
- Turner W (1992) Riot! The Story of the East Lancashire Loom-Breakers in 1826. Preston. Lancashire County Books.
- Waddell P D S (1993). Co-operative Checks. Tickets, Tokens and Coins. Manchester. British Association of Numismatic Societies.
- Walton J K (1995). Co-operation in Lancashire 1844-1924. In North West Labour History.
- Walton J K (1987). Lancashire. A Social History, 1558-1939. Manchester. Manchester University Press.
- Walton J K (2009). The Post-War decline of the British Retail Co-operative Movement: nature, causes and consequences in Consumerism and the Co-operative Movement in Modern British History. Taking Stock. Edited

by Black L and Robertson N. Manchester. Manchester University Press.
- Wilson J F, Webster A and Vorberg-Rugh R (2013). Building Co-operation. A Business History of the Co-operative Group, 1863-2013. Oxford. Oxford Press.
- Winstanley M J (1983). The Shopkeeper's World 1830-1914. Manchester. Manchester University Press.
- Wrigley C (2009). The Commemorative Urge: the Co-operative Movements Collective Memory, in Consumerism and the Co-operative Movement in Modern British History. Taking Stock. Edited by Black L and Robertson N. Manchester. Manchester University Press.

INDEX

A

Abbey Village 135-6.
Accrington 41-2.
Adlington xi, 3, 38, 47, 50, 67, 104-5, 118-22, 132-4,143-4.
Anderton, James 16.
Arkwright, Sir Richard 1-2, 15.
Asting, William 47, 52, 56.
Atherton. 62.

B

Backhouse, H. B. 135-6, 139.
Bacup 41.
Bamber Bridge 2, 30, 39.
Birkacre xii, xiii, 1-3, 7, 9-17, 19-22, 24-5, 48, 78, 99, 127, 138.
Birtwistle, Thomas 69, 75-6, 81.
Blackburn 29, 38, 41, 44-5, 52, 56, 135.
Blacklidge, William 139, 143.
Blackrod 7, 39-40, 118.
Block Printers Union 3, 6, 9, 19, 24.
Bolton 7, 14, 21, 26, 36, 38, 52, 56, 82.
Bolton, Henry 144.

Brindle 30, 132.
Brinscall 3, 135, 137.
Burgh Hall 1, 15-18.
Bury 21, 42, 52, 96.
Butterfield, Jesse 135.

C

Carr, William 47, 75-6, 97, 124.
Carson, William 12-3, 15, 17-21, 23-4.
Cartmell, William 135.
Chadderton 54,72,74.
Charnock Richard 38, 132.
Chartists 28-31, 40, 48, 98.
Christian Socialist 10, 23, 31, 34-6, 40, 44-5, 51.
Chorley Family Funeral and Friendly Assurance Society 25.
Chorley Operative Conservative Association 27.
Chorley Permanent Building Society 62.
Cobbett, William 7-8.
Cobden, Richard 20,63.
Co-operative Wholesale Society (CWS) 34, 59, 74, 88, 107.
Coppull xi, 1, 38, 132,

Cotton Famine 50-1, 55, 79, 93, 104, 114, 135.
Cowling Bridge 2-3, 19.
Critchley, John 107, 112-3, 119-20.
Crompton, Peter 27.
Crosse Hall 19, 48, 55, 84, 104-5, 119-20, 144.
Croston 38, 61, 132.

D

Darwen 79.
Doherty, John xiii, 6-7, 9-10, 24.
Duxbury 30, 132.

E

Eccles, Alfred Ephraim 137-8.
Euxton xi, 50, 104, 132, 143.

F

Fairbrother, Samuel 47-8, 52, 96, 111, 113, 115, 117-8.
Farn, J. C. 40-2.
Firth, Peter xiii, 38, 47-9, 50, 62, 79, 104, 114, 116, 129-30, 133.

G

Garstang, Lawrence 26.
Graham, John 2-3, 20, 23.

H

Handloom Weaving 25, 28, 30, 47, 61, 130, 135, 139-42, 144.
Heapey 56, 91, 132, 138, 141-3.
Hebden Bridge xii, 54, 88.
Heyes, Jim xi, xii, 2, 29-30, 117.
Hirst, Thomas 12-4.

Hodgkinson, Thomas 43, 48, 52, 68, 105, 107, 112-3, 119, 124, 138, 144.
Hoghton 27, 132.
Holyoake, George Jacob xii, 4, 22, 33, 43-4.
Hunt, Henry "Orator" 8.

I

Improvement Commission 38-9, 49, 55, 63, 78, 80, 89, 93-5, 113, 117.

K

Karfoot, Mathias 58, 61-2, 64, 67-8, 70, 84, 92, 108, 129, 143.
Karfoot, William 4, 4-5, 47, 52, 57-8, 61-4, 66-70, 74-85, 89, 92, 94, 96-7, 105, 107, 111, 113, 116, 119, 129, 140, 144.
King, Dr. William 3-4, 33.

L

Lawrence, William 63-4, 79-80, 92, 129.
Leyland 26, 30, 37-8, 123, 132, 134.
Lightoller 8, 49, 98.
Liverpool 15, 21, 23.
Livesey, Joseph 126.
Longton, Frank xii, xiv, 43, 51, 78, 88, 91, 101, 125, 128-9.
Ludlow, J. M. F. 35-6, 44.

M

Manchester vii, 2, 6-7, 10, 14, 36, 40, 43-4, 64, 97, 111, 127.
Marcroft, William 44, 53-4, 72, 74.
Marsden, Richard 28-9.

Master, Rev. J. S. 39.
Mechanics Institute 100.
Mellor, John 2.
Methodists 39, 61, 91, 139.

N

National Association for the Protection of Labour 6-7, 9.
New Harmony 6.
New Lanark 5, 138.
North West of England United Co-operative Company 12-3, 15.

O

O'Connor, Feargus 28.
Oddfellows 36, 45, 64, 104.
Oldham 44, 53-4, 72-5, 81.
Orangemen 92.
Orbiston 6.
Oswaldtwistle 2.
Owen, Robert ix, 5-6, 12, 15, 18-20, 33, 127.

P

Padiham 37.
Pare, William 10.
Park Road 104=5, 116, 120, 124.
Peterloo 8.
Piggot, Ellis 3,6.
Pitman, Henry 48, 66, 114.
Plug Riots 29-30.
Poor Law 26-7, 41, 83, 134.
Powerloom Weavers 8, 36, 48, 56-8, 86, 130.
Preston ix, xiii, 7-8, 26-30, 35, 38, 40, 42, 45, 56, 88, 93, 103.

R

Ralahine 14.
Rigby, Dr. John 48-9, 58, 67, 93, 112-3, 117, 123.
Rigby, Dr. James Morris 48-9, 117.
Rochdale ix, xii, 15, 31-5, 39-44, 52, 54, 95, 100, 116.
Roman Catholicism 1, 36, 130.

S

Scotland 5-6, 32.
Slater, James 104-5, 134.
Smethurst 49, 62, 65, 70.

T

Taylor, Edmund 12, 19-21.
Temperance 27, 34, 61, 68, 91, 110, 113, 119, 137-8, 140.
Thom, John 49.
Tockholes 8.
Todd, Peter 141-3.

U

Ulnes Walton 61, 132.

W

Walton-le-Dale 30.
Watts, Thomas 15-6.
Wheelton 39, 56, 64, 121-2, 132, 138-43.
White Coppice 122, 137-8.
Whittaker, Henry 58, 107.
Wigan 1, 12, 29, 38, 40, 122, 135.
Windsor, John 55-6, 58, 72, 92.
Withnell 38-40, 121-2, 132, 135-7, 139, 144.
Withnell Fold 139, 143.

Whittle-le-Woods xi, 30, 38, 40,
    50, 56, 67-8, 92, 104-5, 119-
    20, 132, 143-5.

Y

Yorkshire 4, 32, 35-6, 41, 79,
    95, 98.

ABOUT THE AUTHOR

John Harrison has lived in Lancashire for over fifty years and for most of that time he has lived in Chorley. For more than a decade he worked as a lecturer in Further Education before spending the rest of his career managing educational provision in local government. Whilst in mid-career, he was fortunate to be able to study for a Masters degree and produced a thesis, *The Development of Medical Care and Public Health in Nineteenth Century Chorley*. Subsequently local history research and writing had to be put on hold whilst the focus was on family and career. Since retiring John has been better able to pursue his passions of research/writing, as well as travel, rambling, family history and music, and until finishing this book, the highlight had been walking Wainwright's Coast to Coast from St. Bees to Robin Hoods Bay.